The War Th~

Anusha Nandakumar ... graduate in film directi~ ... ~n the Satyajit Ray Film and Telev...

She is one of the founders a~ ... of Bharatiya Digital Party—BhaDiPa—a Marathi e~ ...~nment YouTube channel.

Anusha has directed a comedy series called *Pandu* for MX Player and is currently working on her upcoming series, *Radical*, for Endemol Shine.

Her documentary film, *The Boxing Ladies,* won the National Film Award in 2010 and her short films have been screened at various national and international film festivals.

Anusha and Sandeep Saket are the creators and writers of an untitled thriller series for Amazon Prime to be directed by Rohit Shetty.

The War That Made R&AW is her first book.

Sandeep Saket has been working in the Mumbai film and television industry for more than ten years. He graduated in film direction and screenplay writing from the Satyajit Ray Film and Television Institute (SRFTI). His films, made as part of the curriculum at SRFTI, have been screened at various festivals including Belgrade (Serbia), Mumbai International Film Festival, Kolkata International Film Festival, International Film Festival of India in Goa, Twilight International Films Festival and Osian's Cinefan.

He has written the Hindi feature film *Saat Uchakke*, the series *Dilliwood* on MensXP, and is working on series that are in development for various OTT platforms.

The War That Made R&AW is his first book.

THE
WAR
THAT MADE
R&AW

ANUSHA NANDAKUMAR
SANDEEP SAKET

GOLDEN PEN

First published by Westland Publications Private Limited, in association with Golden Pen, in 2021

1st Floor, A Block, East Wing, Plot No. 40, SP Infocity, Dr MGR Salai, Perungudi, Kandanchavadi, Chennai 600096

Westland and the Westland logo are the trademarks of Westland Publications Private Limited, or its affiliates.

ISBN: 9789390679348

Typeset by SÜRYA, New Delhi

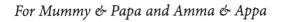

For Mummy & Papa and Amma & Appa

The reason the enlightened prince and the wise general conquer the enemy whenever they move and their achievements surpass those of ordinary men, is foreknowledge.

– Sun Tsu, The Art of War

Contents

Chapter I

The Intelligencer

JAMES BOND IS UNDOUBTEDLY THE MOST FAMOUS fictional secret agent in history. The swashbuckling, glamour-oozing, martini-drinking British spy has made the art of espionage look very easy and very sexy.

Rameshwar Nath Kao, the great Indian spymaster, was as far a cry from the flamboyant Agent 007 as was possible. He lived in the shadows and operated stealthily from them. He knew that, in real life, the worst thing that could happen to a spy, was the revelation of his true identity.

Kao was a visionary who singlehandedly put Indian Intelligence on the world map. It is said that he was a man of few words and someone who preferred to let his work speak for him. 'The life of a spy is to know and not to be known,' was a simple adage of espionage tradecraft that Kao preached all his life. It was this philosophy that helped him lay the foundation stones of India's modern external Intelligence-gathering unit, the Research and Analysis Wing (R&AW), in 1968.

He is the father of modern Indian espionage, and this is the story of how he helped India liberate Bangladesh.

◻

Kao's acumen as an Intelligencer first came into the limelight with the Kashmir Princess probe in 1955.

On 11 April 1955, a chartered Air India plane named Kashmir Princess was on the tarmac of Hong Kong airport, waiting for the arrival of its last passenger. At the scheduled departure time, Captain D.K. Jatar was informed over radio that the VIP passenger had cancelled at the last minute. He was asked to proceed as planned.

Brief pre-flight checks in place, the Kashmir Princess was airborne in about ten minutes.

The plane that Jatar was flying was an American-made Lockheed L-749 Constellation aircraft. Its destination was Jakarta, Indonesia. In addition to the captain, there were seven crew members on the flight. Of the eleven passengers on board, most were Chinese delegates on their way to attend the Bandung Conference. India's first prime minister, Jawaharlal Nehru, along with Indonesian president Sukarno, had initiated this grouping of newly independent Asian and African nations in Bandung. It was to be a precursor to the Non-Aligned Movement, a forum where leaders of the newly formed countries of the developing world were going to pledge to guard their independence. They would steer clear of any allegiance to either of the warring superpowers—the United States and the Soviet Union.

The plane was five hours into its journey and 125 kilometres from the nearest airport when an explosion rocked the cockpit.

The crew members, Indians, barely had a second to react when they saw flames coming out of one of the plane's engines. The pilot noticed that the sign for the fire warning in the baggage compartment had turned on. The aircraft was on fire, the engines were shutting down, and the plane had started a rapid downward spiral. Screams filled the passenger cabin of the aircraft.

Even amidst the chaos, the pilots knew that this was no time to panic. There were lives to be saved. The first thing that the captain did was to send out a distress signal, disclosing the aircraft's current position over the Natuna Islands in the South China Sea. Next, he pushed the throttle and pointed the plane's nose downwards, just as the radio stopped working and the electrical systems started failing. Turning back was not an option and directing the plane into the sea seemed like the best bet to save the passengers. The descent began, and it seemed that they would, after all, be able to save themselves.

However, the fire spread rapidly to the aircraft's critical systems before they hit the water, and the plane exploded mid-air. Blazing, the Kashmir Princess crashed into the sea. Of the nineteen people on board, only three crew members managed to survive.

China and India reacted with horror to the news. But the leaders of both countries had the same thought: Zhou Enlai, the first premier of the People's Republic of China, would be dead right now if circumstances had been different.

Enlai was the VIP passenger scheduled to be on the plane. A last-minute change of plans due to a medical emergency had saved his life.

The first Chinese radio broadcast after the incident said: Sabotage. There was every reason to suspect that this was an attempt to subvert the fledgling India–China relationship. Premier Enlai turned to Nehru for assistance, insisting that India become a part of the investigation.

In the 1950s, China's relationship with Hong Kong, still a British colony, was tumultuous. Enlai did not trust the British, and his distrust extended to Hong Kong Intelligence. Since the plane had taken off from Hong Kong, Enlai strongly believed that Hong Kong and Britain were tied into the conspiracy.

Apart from the close relationship that the two leaders shared, Nehru felt that India was obligated to step in. The aircraft as well as the crew in question were Indian, and thus, there was more at stake for India in this matter than a political friendship.

He instructed Bhola Nath Mullick, then head of the Intelligence Bureau (IB), to put his best man on the job. This investigation was a glamorous 'special assignment', involving international leaders. All the top agents at the IB hankered for the job. Still, the most deserving man that Mullick could think of was thirty-seven-year-old Rameshwar Nath Kao, affectionately nicknamed Ramji.

◻

R.N. Kao was born in Benaras to a Kashmiri Pandit family in 1918. He joined the United Provinces Cadre of the Indian Imperial Police (the Indian Police Service after Independence) in 1940. After Independence, he was transferred to the IB—India's oldest Intelligence agency, formed in London in 1887 and recast in 1947 as the Central Intelligence Bureau under the Ministry of Home Affairs.

One of the principal tasks assigned to Kao at IB in those days was VIP security. In this role, he had handled the security detail for Nehru himself. Kao was also in charge of VIP security for foreign dignitaries visiting India. It was the training that he received in this capacity that prepared him for this, his first major assignment: the 1955 Kashmir Princess probe in Beijing, formerly known as Peking.

Kao knew he had been handpicked to lead the investigation and was well aware of the magnitude of the task that lay ahead of him. The eyes of China, Hong Kong, the UK and India were on him. It was his first 'special assignment' and the pressure was tremendous, even for the usually imperturbable Kao.

At the Beijing airport, the immigration officer asked Kao how long his visit was going to be. Kao told the officer that he would be staying a few weeks, not knowing at the time that the investigation would stretch on for almost half a year.

At the Chinese premier's office in Beijing, Kao's one-on-one briefing with Zhou Enlai was held behind closed doors. Even though Kao was determined to be the neutral investigator on the case, Enlai advanced theories of a Taiwanese conspiracy behind the crash and urged Kao to expedite the investigation process and submit his findings.

Little did Kao realise, as he took on the assignment, that he was going to be caught up in the crossfire of the internal politics between China, Hong Kong and Britain. From the outset, the case was rife with complications. The plane had taken off from Hong Kong, and it had crashed into Indonesian waters. The aircraft had been built in the US but was owned by

India. The people aboard who had died in the crash were all Chinese. Hence, de facto, five countries—the UK, Indonesia, the US, India and China—became part of the investigation. And it fell to Kao to navigate this very complex political labyrinth in order to find out the truth.

Over several months, Kao worked doggedly in collaboration with the Chinese, Hong Kong and British police to unravel the threads of the conspiracy. The investigation took him to Singapore, Indonesia, the Philippines, Hong Kong and China. His diplomatic demeanour allowed him to investigate freely and build strong friendships, particularly with MI4, British Intelligence, who were posted in Hong Kong and Indonesia at the time. While forging these connections, Kao was unaware that in the future they would be instrumental in the formation of R&AW.

Throughout this period, Kao was all alone in foreign lands, with no real ally. The language, food, customs and traditions were strange and alienating. However, he did not allow himself to succumb to any kind of pressure, internal or external. He knew he had to finish what he had started. A thorough professional, he painstakingly put together an exhaustive file on the investigation and his findings. Every detail, however minor, was recorded, every lead followed up on, and every fact corroborated.

His patience and rigour finally paid off in September 1955. A clear picture had started emerging of the events that had occurred on the day of the Kashmir Princess crash. Realising that he had finished his probe, Kao sent an official message to Enlai with his investigative results. In Beijing, Enlai immediately sent for Kao.

In a detailed briefing, Kao told Enlai how his investigation had led him to Chou Chu. A Taiwanese national working as a member of the ground maintenance crew of the Hong Kong Aircraft Engineering Company, Chu had agreed to place a time bomb—a weapon of choice in those days—in the Kashmir Princess. In return, he was promised a reward of 6,00,000 Hong Kong dollars.

The mastermind behind the plot was Chiang Kai-shek, an ousted Chinese leader, who had gone on to become the ruler of Taiwan. Kai-shek was plotting to kill Zhou Enlai, and when it was publicly known that he would be taking a chartered flight from Hong Kong to attend the Bandung Conference, he made his move. The Kashmir Princess crash was the result of this ongoing political rivalry between China and Taiwan.

Enlai was highly impressed with the conduct of Kao's investigation, including the dexterity of his mediations between the colonial government in Hong Kong and the communist government in mainland

China. To show his appreciation, Enlai rewarded Kao with his coveted personal seal, an honour reserved for the most deserving public servants in the Chinese republic.

Kao came back to India a true hero in December 1955.

□

In the same year that the Kashmir Princess went down, Indira Gandhi started her political career as a member of the working committee of the Congress party. At the time, neither Kao nor Indira Gandhi had any way of knowing that their paths would cross and that they would play critical roles in the birthing of a new nation in the Indian subcontinent.

In 1956, Kao resumed his duties as the chief security head for Nehru. He spent two uneventful years in India, immersed in his job and working to strengthen India's internal Intelligence unit. He also settled into the rhythm of family life. He was married to Malini, the daughter of Justice Tej Narain Mulla of Allahabad. A daughter, Achla, was born to them.

In 1958, he was sent on another special assignment to Ghana. It proved to be a critical mission for Kao—one that would test his mettle and grit, moulding him into the man who would shape the future of Intelligence-gathering in India.

The Ghana chapter in Kao's life had its genesis in the year of India's independence. In 1947, India was starting a new epoch in its history. At the same time, in the Gold Coast, an African colony under British rule, a political party called the United Gold Coast Convention began agitating for self-governance. After ten long and hard years, in 1957, the British government finally gave up its control over the region. The Gold Coast was renamed Ghana, an independent republic, with Kwame Nkrumah as its first prime minister.

Freedom and self-determination, however, do not come easy. Like India, Ghana too struggled to stand on its own feet after independence. It soon realised that if it wanted to advance in the world, it would need a reliable Intelligence apparatus.

Ghana had been part of the Bandung Conference in 1955. It had formed close ties with India because of their shared history of struggle against the British. In his hour of need, in 1958, Nkrumah turned to Nehru, relying on their warm, personal friendship. He wanted to set up an Intelligence agency in Ghana. Nehru, in turn, turned to Bhola Nath Mullick from the IB, who recommended Kao for the job. Kao, who was joint director of IB at the time, had earned Mullick's respect and recommendation for this vital task largely due to the success of the Kashmir Princess probe.

Nehru proposed a three-pronged strategy to Nkrumah for setting up a Ghanaian Intelligence agency. It was decided that Mullick would first visit Ghana and prepare a detailed plan after assessing the situation there. Two Ghanaians would then be given training in India by the IB. Subsequently, an Indian expert, Kao, would be sent to Ghana for a year to set the wheels in motion.

Nkrumah promptly accepted the scheme outlined by Nehru. In April 1958, he sent two trusted officers, Paul Yankee and Ben Forjoe, from the Bureau of National Investigations, then known as the Special Branch, to India for training with the IB.

Kao left for Ghana in February 1959. Operating out of Accra, the nation's capital, he worked there for a year. To begin with, he did not even have an office table, let alone qualified personnel. He had to set everything up from scratch, building up the basic framework and infrastructure of the country's Intelligence apparatus. But the Ghanaians assigned to Kao at Accra were a cheerful lot. They were eager to learn and extremely devoted to Nkrumah and their country.

After a year of dedicated hard work, despite minimal funds and the complete absence of a trained workforce, Kao succeeded in establishing the Foreign Service Research Bureau (FSRB), Ghana's external and internal Intelligence agency. The FSRB was the first foray made by an Indian Intelligence officer at a global level. Kao saw his stint in Ghana as an opportunity to use his newly developed methodology and international experience in Intelligence and counter-Intelligence.

Kao was called back to India in December 1959 by Mullick to resume his work at the IB, and another officer was selected to go to Ghana in Kao's stead.

The officer who would replace Kao in Ghana was Kinattinkara Sankaran Nair. A few years younger than Kao, he had already made a name for himself as a fiercely dedicated and exceptionally sharp Intelligence officer. He had started out as a law student but abandoned his studies midway when he was inducted into the Indian Imperial Police. From there, he had made his way to the IB, where he stayed on after Independence.

Back in his IB office, Kao was winding up for the day one evening when there was a knock on his door. Even before he looked up to see who it was, he could tell from the brisk *rat-a-tat-tat* that the knocker was a precise person. Kao had a fair idea of who it might be.

'If I may disturb you for a minute or two—' The officer began, but abruptly stopped. 'Oh, I am so sorry. I did not know that you were leaving for the day!'

'Not even the best of spies can be expected to know that, Nair,' Kao said, smiling. 'It is Nair, isn't it?'

Sankaran Nair returned the smile, and Kao perceived that his colleague was brimming with the same nervous excitement that he had felt when he was about to leave for China. The debut overseas assignment always brings with it a fair amount of nervousness. Clearly, Nair wanted Kao's insights for Ghana before he left for the assignment.

'Espionage is quite a lonely business of selling lies, my friend,' Kao advised. 'The only way to succeed in it is by honing your salesmanship.'

The Ghana assignment forged a strong bond of trust and friendship between Kao and Nair. Their personalities were like chalk and cheese, nevertheless, their natures complemented each other, and they got along splendidly. Kao was soft-spoken, a teetotaller, and liked to keep to himself. Nair was tough as nails, flamboyant, outspoken, and knew how to get the job done.

In Ghana, Nair lovingly nurtured the FSRB that Kao had built from scratch. The years 1959 and 1960 became important milestones for both these gentlemen. When Kao established R&AW in 1968, Nair became his able deputy, helping the institution to grow and flourish in its fledgling years.

Chapter 2

Neighbourly Love

THE BIBLE TELLS US TO LOVE OUR NEIGHBOURS AS well as to love our enemies. And usually, they are the same people.

It was with this message that P.N. Haksar summoned Kao for an urgent meeting with Prime Minister Indira Gandhi in 1968. Anybody else would have wondered what Haksar was talking about, but Kao knew precisely what he meant.

A powerful bureaucrat whom Indira Gandhi held in very high regard, P.N. Haksar was the prime minister's principal advisor and a close confidante. She consulted him on most matters of policy and statecraft.

Kao had been in London, attending a rather dull conference. He abandoned the conference mid-way and returned to India on the next available flight.

It had been thirteen years since Kao had made a name for himself in the Kashmir Princess probe. Over the years, he had made silent but significant contributions to the still-evolving world of Indian Intelligence.

Kao had a fair idea why the prime minister had summoned him that day. He suspected it had to do with India's humiliating defeat in the war of 1962 against China and Kao's report on the same.

In 1954, Mao Zedong became the chairman of the People's Republic of China. During his regime, China's relations with India deteriorated due to the dispute over the Aksai Chin region of Kashmir. India and China both claimed proprietorship of the area, which was effectively in Chinese control. The strain on bilateral relations increased in 1959 when Nehru granted asylum to His Holiness the Dalai Lama who was fleeing from the Chinese People's Liberation Army's onslaught in Tibet.

The 1962 war—in which 1,383 Indian soldiers were killed, 1,047 were wounded, and nearly 4,000 were captured, all during the short period of a month—showed India how ill-equipped it was, both in terms of combat and Intelligence. It was clear that Indian Intelligence had completely failed to predict the oncoming Chinese attack. India's defeat also drove home the fact that a country's Intelligence agency could not depend on foreign agencies for critical information in times of war. At the time, the IB's foreign Intelligence arm was almost non-existent and India had failed to build on the hard Intelligence provided by its field operatives. Instead, it had relied heavily on friendly Western agencies for information. These agencies had only reaffirmed India's own belief that China would not engage in an armed conflict.

After the war, India realised that 'Intelligence' is a long-term process of safe-guarding one's country. It was essential to keep a watch on the neighbours not only during wartime but in peacetime as well. And this would require the restructuring and revitalisation of the existing Indian Intelligence system.

At that time, the IB's responsibilities were limited to gathering domestic Intelligence and dealing with internal security. India's crushing defeat in the war prompted the bureau to create a specialised wing to gather external Intelligence and to perform covert operations on neighbouring countries. This was the genesis of the Aviation Research Centre (ARC), the Special Frontier Force (SFF) or Establishment 22, and the Special Service Bureau or the Sashastra Seema Bal (SSB). The ARC was an aviation wing with sophisticated technical Intelligence-gathering capabilities for special operations. The SFF was the 'stay-behind organisation'[1]

---

[1] In a stay-behind operation, a country retains secret operatives or organisations in its own territory in case an enemy occupies that territory. In such an event, the operatives would form the basis of a resistance movement or act as spies.

for the Indo-Tibetan Border Police, which operated on the Sino-Indian border, with political and security duties. The SSB supplied armed support for espionage and would later provide the same for R&AW.

Kao was named director for the ARC. The ARC was designed to be the game-changer for Indian Intelligence. However, in 1964, not even a year into its existence, it suffered its first significant setback. China secretly conducted two nuclear tests in its Xinjiang province, becoming the first Asian country to go nuclear. This development caught the world unawares and came as a shock to India. Their hostile neighbour had, with no forewarning, assumed the status of a nuclear-weapon state.

At this juncture, China had started to become a problem for the US too, because it posed a direct threat to the power dynamics of the existing world order. India and the US reached an agreement to collaborate on a clandestine operation to keep an eye on China's nuclear activity. They planned to install a nuclear-powered sensing device on India's second-highest peak, Nanda Devi. As the head of the ARC, Kao was contacted by the Central Intelligence Agency (CIA)—the civilian foreign Intelligence service of the federal government of the US—to oversee this operation. To be conducted by a combined team of the CIA and the IB, the mission was code-named 'Operation HAT'.

A joint mountaineering expedition was launched under the leadership of Captain Manmohan Singh Kohli to install the radioactive device on the peak. The nuclear-powered device could detect even the lightest seismic activity caused by nuclear explosions in China. The expedition went smoothly and the crew had nearly reached their destination when a terrible blizzard waylaid them. Kohli had to choose between his men and the machine. He chose his men; they could always mount another operation to install the device. They abandoned the device, planning to return in more favourable weather to retrieve and install it. Over the next few years, several expeditions were mounted to retrieve the device, but it was never found.

Operation HAT was one of ARC's earliest trysts in the game of Intelligence. Though the mission was a failure, Kao learned a great deal about professionalism, planning and covert operations from the CIA.

◻

In August 1965, another incident caught India by surprise. The IB failed to foresee Pakistan's plans to start an armed insurgency in Kashmir. Around 30,000 Pakistani Army soldiers, dressed as Kashmiri locals, infiltrated the Indian territory of Kashmir; the aim was to attack by infiltration and resolve their decades-old conflict with India over the Kashmir territory.

This mission was named Operation Gibraltar by then president of Pakistan, Ayub Khan, inspired by the eighth-century Muslim conquest of Spain that had been initiated from the port of Gibraltar. He believed that a well-trained, irregular force would weaken India's resolve and bring the conflict to a conference table without provoking a war.

Indian authorities were informed of this plan by some Kashmiri locals who identified and caught a few of the Pakistani Army personnel. Operation Gibraltar triggered the war of 1965 between India and Pakistan.

Even after the war had begun, the IB failed to predict the massive build-up of Pakistani armoured divisions in Kashmir's Chhamb sector. Indian troops became aware of the presence of the enemy only when rockets and shells rained down on them in a surprise attack. The Indian Army, however, fought back valiantly and managed to repulse the attack. They not only drove the enemy back but also launched several successful attacks on Pakistan.

The conflict lasted twenty-two days, at the end of which India captured 1,920 square kilometres of Pakistani territory, including the strategically crucial Haji Pir Pass. The war ended in Pakistan's decisive tactical and strategic defeat.

Before India could enjoy the victory, however, Lal Bahadur Shastri, who was Prime Minister at the time, frittered these military gains away at the negotiating table in the Tashkent Declaration of 1965—a peace agreement signed by the leaders of the two countries post the war. A furious and shocked Indian Army could only sit and watch as every square inch that they had fought for over twenty-two days was given away by Lal Bahadur Shastri in the six-day negotiation leading up to the Declaration.

The euphoria at defeating Pakistan in the war was quickly replaced by recrimination about faulty Intelligence before and during the conflict.

Kao had had a ringside view during both wars. During this period, he had been following the Ayub Khan regime in Pakistan very carefully and had taken note of the problems that the country was facing, especially the rising conflict between East and West Pakistan. The ruling factions of the two territories were growing apart at a fast pace.

Learning from the failures of the 1965 war, Kao started etching out a bigger Intelligence plan. He knew that Intelligence agencies would keep getting created, merged and dissolved, but without the right thought process, it would all be for nought. Kao was well aware that Intelligence agencies needed to be backed by someone at the top. Looking at the bigger picture, he discerned that the IB's setbacks were a consequence of the incapability of bureaucrats to take quick actions and assume leadership. He firmly believed that the time was ripe for action, and every second that was wasted would lead to the loss of a once-in-a-lifetime opportunity. Over several weeks, Kao typed out a detailed report and came up with a plan.

After Lal Bahadur Shastri's unexpected death in 1966, Indira Gandhi had assumed the post of prime minister. Putting his trust in his acquaintance with her father and their relationship of mutual respect, Kao reached out directly to Indira Gandhi with his report, hoping that it would set things in motion. All he had ever wanted was for India to be adequately equipped to face any kind of internal or external threat, be it war or political subversion. Haksar's phone call summoning Kao to meet Indira Gandhi had led him to hope that he could finally transform his dream into concrete action.

□

As Kao waited to be summoned into the prime minister's chambers, he knew that it all rested on the decision of the woman who sat on the other side of the wall—Indira Gandhi.

It had been two years since Indira Gandhi had assumed the prime minister's post. Ever since she had been elected, Gandhi had sensed, in most people around her, a feeling that she had only inherited the

throne because she was Nehru's daughter. Even after
her election, the 'right-wing' faction of her party, led
by Morarji Desai, kept up its onslaught against her.

It also took her very little time to conclude that
the IB was not a sufficient safeguard against external
threats. As prime minister, she had visited the US
and the Soviet Union, and the Intelligence-gathering
activity she had observed in these countries had made
her realise that international espionage would only get
more significant with time.

Conflict is the very essence of human nature, and
as men fight, so do countries. The greatest power
that one country can wield over another is sensitive
information. Which is why espionage is an age-old
tradition.

Kao was certainly a credit to his profession. His
report lay in front of Indira Gandhi as she sat in
her chambers, contemplating her decision. It was
not merely a detailed plan to strengthen external
Intelligence-gathering for the country, but also a
comprehensive vision statement for India's future
Intelligence agencies. Over the last few months, Gandhi
had read it several times and was highly impressed by
the plan.

Gandhi's admiration stemmed from the sheer
brilliance of the proposal as well as the ambitious
scope of Kao's imagination. He wanted the new

agency to be of the calibre of the famed CIA. The sheer scale of the plan was daunting, but Gandhi knew that it was the right time to implement it. She had already discussed and debated it with her coterie of ministers.

P.N. Haksar, who had also gone through the report several times, allayed the prime minister's apprehensions about the viability of the plan. He reinforced her belief that India needed a strong external Intelligence wing. Indira Gandhi trusted Haksar implicitly. She knew he always spoke his mind to her regardless of any differences of opinion or ideology they might have.

However, she faced internal opposition from Y.B. Chavan, then home minister, who was a very powerful man in the Cabinet. Chavan had served as defence minister of India (1962–66), and after the 1965 war, he had commissioned a paper recommending the formation of a new military Intelligence agency consisting of army officers and academics from various fields. This paper had become the basis of Gandhi's current decision. She was quite sure that she did not want a replica of the IB. All modern democratic nations had separate external and internal Intelligence agencies. The rationale was that the basic requirements, including the nature of personnel for these agencies, differed.

Gandhi could not help but marvel at the sheer ineptitude she had been witnessing ever since the Pakistan debacle. Intelligence failures happen everywhere, including developed countries. But they were acknowledged and corrected. This, however, had not happened in India, with the focus being on sweeping the dirt under the carpet.

Gandhi had finally decided that the IB was incapable of running foreign missions, and certainly not missions of the magnitude that Kao had in mind. Ever since she had reached this conclusion, the prime minister had been racking her brains for a solution. Now she believed she had one, and hence, Kao was sitting in the waiting room outside her office. Taking a deep breath, she rang the bell on her table and asked for Kao to be escorted into her chambers.

What happened behind closed doors during that meeting will perhaps stay a secret forever. What has, however, fallen through the cracks over time indicates that Kao was reasonably aware of what Gandhi had in mind and had his own demands ready. Anyone who knew Kao would have expected nothing less from a man of his stature and astuteness.

During the closed-door conversation between Kao and Gandhi, Kao's plan was again carefully dissected, questioned and analysed. Gandhi had reached her conclusion. A new agency was needed, one that would work under her direct supervision, answering to no one else. She wanted Kao to head it. It was unprecedented, they both agreed, but also completely necessary and far beyond the capabilities of the IB. Indira Gandhi told Kao that she did not want the IB functioning to be replicated in the new agency—in other words, old wine in a new bottle. She was entrusting Kao with the creation of the new agency, she said, and he could run it the way he deemed fit, but for a few conditions. Firstly, Gandhi wanted the organisation to be multifaceted and integrated. The organisation would amalgamate information using technology, infrastructure, analytics and data sources across agencies. Secondly, she did not want Kao to recruit exclusively from the IPS. She also stipulated that the top two posts would be filled at the discretion of the prime minister.

Apart from the conditions laid down by Gandhi, Kao demanded complete carte blanche with regard to recruitment as well as the running of the organisation. It was granted immediately. Kao also put forth a request to bring in officers from the IB. Gandhi replied, 'Ramji, what I want from the new bureau is for it to be a formidable Intelligence-gathering agency, a force to reckon with. All foreign desks from IB move with you. Two hundred and fifty personnel from IB will be transferred to the new bureau. And a budget of twenty lakh rupees will be sanctioned. Haksar saab will guide you through this.'

Rules and policies, which would be refined over the next few months, had already been drawn up by Kao based on detailed studies of the CIA, MI6, Israel's Mossad, France's Direction Générale de la Sécurité Extérieure, and Japan's Public Security Intelligence Agency.

It was a momentous day, and Indira Gandhi had taken a monumental decision.

Chapter 3

The Kaoboys

HAVING SECURED SUPPORT FROM THE TOP ECHELONS of the government, Kao started the vital process of putting his core team together. The first man on his list was Sankaran Nair.

'R-A-W. RAW? What kind of name is that?' asked Nair, incredulous.

Kao corrected him. 'It's R&AW, Research and Analysis Wing.' He joked, 'We will be able to "research" as much as we want to. Cabinet Secretary D.S. Joshi has come up with this name. We will be attached as a wing of the cabinet secretariat. It's a good front.'

'So, agencies of other countries get "intelligence" in their names, while we will have to manage with "research"?' Nair said with a chuckle. He added, 'Anyway, to quote Shakespeare, what's in a name?'

In all the years that Kao had worked with Sankaran Nair, he had never known him to mince words. However, Nair's rough and tough attitude, which was in stark contrast to Kao's refined persona, did not stand in the way of his getting results where work was concerned. Kao believed in soothing words and smiling faces, while Nair believed not only in calling a spade a spade but in picking it up and belligerently waving it in the other person's face. Nair had many qualities, but patience with fools was not one of them.

Nair had an unfailing sense of conviction in his work. Following the 1965 Indo-Pakistan war, a commission was set up to investigate the allegations of IB's inefficiency. Nair was a member of the commission. He submitted sixty-five acerbically worded reports to the investigating committee, outlining in painful detail where his agency had fallen short. When it came to the security and integrity of his country, Nair had no tolerance for laggards—friendships and office politics be damned. It was this attitude that Kao was relying on, to shape the uncut stone of R&AW into the diamond that it needed to become.

However, Kao was also aware that Nair's induction into R&AW was not going to earn him any friends within the IB. The agency had dealt with a great deal of severe criticism after the Indo-Pakistan war in 1965. There was no doubt that the advent of a rival agency, merely three years later, was going to trigger many a fraying temper in the IB hierarchy.

Kao had brought up this point in his meeting with Indira Gandhi two weeks earlier.

'I did not think you concerned yourself with trifles such as childish envies, Mr Kao,' Gandhi had said with a smile.

'You know I do not, madam,' Kao replied, 'but my headaches are ultimately going to be your headaches if we do this.'

'Then let them be my headaches,' Gandhi had said. 'You tell me what you need.'

Kao had rattled off a list of things. Gandhi tilted her head and approved all of them in a heartbeat. In those early days, Haksar was Kao's guiding light. He stood staunchly by Kao's side, helping him navigate bureaucracy and politics, and ensuring that he was able to access the infrastructure he needed to get R&AW up and running. It was also Haksar who had pushed for making Kao the head of R&AW, a 'secretary' under the Prime Minister's Office (PMO). In administrative circles, 'secretary' was a potent title, as a person who held this post could make decisions regarding policy and operations without having to follow long and tedious bureaucratic processes. This meant that Kao could take immediate decisions, financial or otherwise, regarding matters related to the functioning of the agency. In comparison, the head of IB was a 'director', a title which held no such powers.

The R&AW would always remain indebted to Haksar. He not only helped R&AW stand on its feet but gave it wings as well.

'It will be just like Ghana all over again,' Kao told Nair.

'It is not going to be like Ghana, Ramji,' Nair grunted. 'It is going to be much tougher.'

Kao told Nair the reason for the inception of R&AW and about his plans for the agency. With all the trouble brewing in the political climates of their immediate neighbours in the subcontinent, all eyes were on India, and Kao believed that if India wanted to be taken seriously in the arena of global Intelligence, the time to act was now.

'Shanks, would you join me in this task?' Kao asked. 'I know the new boss of the IB has denied you your rightful promotion. I have not got an equivalent rank in the organisation, but I shall try my best to get it for you.'[2] It took Nair less than a second to agree. The proposed role in R&AW was what he had been itching to do in the IB. 'To hell with rank!' Nair exclaimed.

The next man on Kao's wish list was P.N. Banerjee.

Banerjee was an ex-army officer from West Bengal. Kao estimated that his rigorous military training and experience, combined with his Bengali origins, made

---

[2] K. Sankaran Nair, *Inside IB and RAW: The Rolling Stone that Gathered Moss* (Manas Publications, New Delhi, 2019), pp. 155, 164.

him a perfect fit for the East Pakistan desk. He would be able to execute with ease tasks like on-ground operations, agent handling, liaising with political leaders, and communicating with the locals.

'Mujibur Rahman needs to be given all the support that we can afford,' Banerjee said, his mind working furiously.

'That is your desk,' Kao replied. 'Anyone affected by Ayub Khan's regime, particularly in East Pakistan, is a potential asset.'

Banerjee went on to become the mastermind of critical operations during the Indo-Pakistan war of 1971. He would reach out to the right people and make friends with the true knights in East Pakistan's game of power.

One by one, the other members of R&AW's core team were also carefully handpicked by Kao himself. These gentlemen would go on to display the exceptional discipline and mental strength that was required in the fledgling years of R&AW, especially while dealing with the IB's hostility.

Maj. I.S. Hassanwalia (retd.) braved the ill-will of M.M. Hooja, then director of the IB, and monitored the setting up of R&AW's office on Lodhi Road. Navigating the feud, not unlike a family splitting the spoils after a bitter partition, Hassanwalia procured the building, furniture, accounts staff and food personnel from the IB.

While the logistics were being taken care of, Kao turned his attention to advanced technological means of obtaining direct access to sensitive information. He needed someone to set up the most crucial division at R&AW—the telecommunication and technical monitoring department. He found that expert in Brigadier M.B.K. Nair (retd.). Under his leadership, this department would go on to change the face of Indian Intelligence.

Kao wanted monitoring stations of R&AW set up at all border checkposts and even inside the territories of neighbouring countries. These stations would be supported by the technically advanced satellite monitoring unit, a new and sophisticated technology at the time. The monitoring stations would help to intercept communication between East and West Pakistan as well as other neighbours. The then director general of All India Radio (AIR) joined R&AW as a consultant for this task. The satellite monitoring unit was being honed to become the agency's ears, to eavesdrop on the country's neighbours and alert R&AW during any crisis.

The team, the infrastructure and the plan all came together and the R&AW came into being on 21 September 1968.

■

The birth of R&AW resembled the completion of a complex puzzle. The core team Kao gathered around him had painstakingly helped him bring it together. Sankaran Nair, M.B.K. Nair, I.S. Hassanwalia and P. N. Banerjee were some of his frontmen.

One of the rules that Kao had insisted upon during the formation of the agency was that nothing be written down. Even the status reports prepared for the prime minister would be typed out based on memory, and the document would be hand-delivered to Gandhi by Kao himself. The rule was implicit—no copies, no rough notes, no trail. Hence, when Kao called for a meeting with his core team, the visual was contrary to the popular image of a meeting between high-ranking Intelligence officers. There were no large boards with writing all over them, no notepads strewn on the table, and no files stacked on top of each other. It was just the spies and the spymaster, discussing strategy.

'Knowledge is power,' Kao said in one of the early meetings, addressing the core team assembled in front of him. 'and the proverb holds true for Intelligence agencies more than any other entity. Where the IB failed, we have to succeed.'

The one thing that the new agency absolutely could not afford was to become a cheap knock-off of the IB.

'Unlike the IB, R&AW will dedicate time to asset building,' declared Kao.

Agents and on-ground informers are the assets of an Intelligence agency. They eventually become windows into foreign and enemy territories. HUMINT (human intelligence) is of utmost importance, Kao stressed. A spy would be able to gather information, interpret it in terms of threat perception and transmit it back home in a way that no machine or device—however technologically advanced—ever could.

The days of slipping currency notes to poor villagers living along the border in exchange for information were fast fading away, for the simple reason that those methods could not penetrate deep into enemy territory. The R&AW would rely heavily on the presence of foot soldiers or agents on the ground. These soldiers would deal not in blood and bone but in knowledge. Every titbit, every scrap of information picked up from the ground, would be another brick in the edifice of national Intelligence.

At R&AW, it would be imperative for anyone joining the team to unlearn what they already knew. The Intelligence game that Kao had in mind was unlike any that had been played in the country before. The risks involved were going to be tremendous, the stakes sky-high. For a spy, it was not just the potential risk of losing one's life that was involved. It was also a question of giving up one's identity completely. It was a selfless and instinctive game, played for the love of one's motherland.

And the man who played it best was sitting in that room with Kao—Sankaran Nair.

Operationally, no one in the organisation could match Sankaran Nair. He had been given charge of the West Pakistan desk in R&AW, and had years of experience working the Pakistan desk at the IB. He also commanded much respect abroad, in the shadowy international world of spooks. Sankaran Nair was a man with multiple aliases. He loved the thrill of clandestine operations on the ground. He had mastered the art of reconnoitre and making contacts. He was adept in the infiltration and exfiltration of field agents. He knew how to run agents without even meeting them. There were rumours that Nair had an asset who was highly placed in the Pakistani administration. However, no one could know for sure.

R&AW's first recruits would be operating in neighbouring countries under the cover of Indian embassies. Foreign Secretary T.N. Kaul was to create new jobs at various embassies. The ultimate goal was to have Indian agents set up and run their own networks of informers, moles or operatives overseas.

'Phase 1 would be information gathering or COMINT—communications intelligence. The technology, the foot soldiers and the agents will all contribute to that,' Kao said. 'But the hard work does not end there. We would need a capable team to decipher and analyse all the information coming through.'

Kao told his men that he envisioned a large team consisting of financial and economic analysts, scientists in space technology, as well as agents working on information security and energy security.

'Do not forget Dr Phadke,' M.B.K. Nair chipped in. Brig. Nair had chalked out a network of wireless connections in every part of the world with the help of his assistant Dr Phadke. He would liaise with the Cryptography Division, headed by a cryptography expert who had been transferred to R&AW from the IB.

Brig. Nair spoke about his plans. 'We will train foreign Intelligence recruits in wire-tapping via wireless or telephone using a bug. With this method, we hope our agents will be able to infiltrate and obtain information from Nepal, Bangladesh, Pakistan, Iran, Southeast Asia, and Africa.'

Hassanwalia was curious. 'And how will they communicate with us?'

'Morse code,' Brig. Nair replied. 'Needless to say, this is very risky and will have to be done in absolute secrecy.' He even joked, 'If we can organise a team of operators who speak Tamil and Malayalam, we can communicate via open channels in those languages and no one will know.'

The men in the room burst into hearty laughter.

Apart from the technical and operational details, Kao had something else in mind that he believed would complement the agency's information-gathering strategies.

'Psy-war?' Banerjee asked, curious.

'Psy-ops,' Kao said. 'Psychological operations.' He looked at Banerjee and said with a smile, 'Psychological warfare is essentially information management. With the leeway that the prime minister has given us, we will be able to handle the information that comes in and manipulate and share only what we want with the media. We can ensure that the international spotlight is drawn to topics in favour of the country.'

While the information network would secure India's position in the world dynamics, Kao had also planned to tap into the excellent rapport he had built with his counterparts in various other countries over the years. Mossad could open doors for them with information about West Asia and North Africa. The KGB—the main security agency for the Soviet Union— could help with the supply of arms and ammunition for operations. The CIA too could be of help. Kao's relationship with the CIA had developed after India's war with China in 1962. CIA instructors had trained the SFF, or the secret and elite commando training programme for Tibetan refugees in India, designed to fight the Chinese Army in Tibet. A sizeable portion of the special force consisted of Tibetan rebels. The CIA and Kao discussed the possibility of SFF operating as R&AW's paramilitary unit and being intimately incorporated in the agency's plans. The SFF had since been transferred to R&AW and was now working on the eastern borders of India. Its commando forces were agile and able, and completely at the disposal of R&AW.

The wheels of R&AW were thus set in motion. A rough training module had been finalised. The criteria to look out for in potential recruits had been drawn up. Red flags when screening candidates were listed out. Safe houses to conduct the training of the recruits were identified. Nothing was recorded in writing. Everything was memorised.

Kao's dream was slowly becoming a reality. R&AW was now ready to roll.

Chapter 4

Insertion

THERE WERE THREE MEN IN THE ROOM.

The first was pacing the length of the room at an unsteady pace, his arms swinging wildly.

The second was sitting on a chair, one hand holding a pencil which he tapped rapidly on the table in front of him, and the other holding a phone. He stared unblinkingly at the phone.

The third was sitting in an easy chair, comfortable and relaxed, one leg crossed over the other, having a cup of hot tea and occasionally glancing out of the window. Needless to say, the third man was R.N. Kao.

The three men had been up all night, but it was Kao's two subordinates who looked the worse for wear.

The night had been a critical one, not just for the three of them, but for the entire agency. It was the culmination of nine months of hard work which had begun with the involvement of around twenty people and ultimately boiled down to the three men in the room.

That night, after months of training and preparation, they were about to insert an agent into Pakistan.

◻

His real name was never revealed. He went by the name of Kashmir Bedi, and just like the valley he was named after, the man was amazingly resilient. He had caught the eye of a recruiter, a field agent from Army Intelligence, when he was enjoying kahwa with a group of Muslim boys in a locality close to his own in Punjab. In those days, India's border states— Punjab, Rajasthan, Kashmir and Bengal—were good hunting grounds for recruiting ground assets. It had been twenty-two years since Partition, but there were not too many cultural-linguistic differences between the two countries yet. R&AW recruiters had found it relatively easy to identify and recruit people from these states to train for infiltration into Pakistan on Intelligence-gathering missions.

The agent noticed that the young man mingled easily, had a way with words, and possessed a disarming personality that could lower the other person's guard within minutes. The recruiter had been looking for a young man like him, one who had an eye for detail and a nose for gossip. Bedi was quietly placed under surveillance.

The field agent watched Kashmir Bedi for over a month while other agents at R&AW conducted a thorough background check on his family, friends, romantic interests, enemies, adventures and misadventures. Every little detail had been sniffed out before the recruiter even approached Bedi.

The first approach was always the trickiest. Once the recruiter made contact, he had only the duration of that meeting to decide if the candidate was the right one. If he or she turned out to be unsuitable, or worse, a Pakistani spy, the recruiter could end up with a huge target painted on his back. On the other hand, if the candidate did turn out to be the right one, then there would be no time to lose. This recruit then had to be uprooted from his natural habitat and put in an isolated environment, where he would be moulded and shaped into a different person. It was his performance in the R&AW training that would determine how he could be of use to the agency and decide the future of the spy.

When it came to recruiting new on-ground assets, recruiters were taught that most agents were motivated by one or more of these: money, ideology, coercion or ego (in short, MICE). Bedi, it turned out, was a patriot. The recruiter told him what he had in mind for him, and that he would have to go to Pakistan within the next two months. Bedi considered the offer for about two minutes before accepting it.

Contrary to popular perception, Intelligence agencies do not hate the portrayal of spies in films and popular fiction. They let writers create an aura of glamour around the fictional portrayals of spies for the world to savour while they work quietly in the shadows, thankful that their actual methods and operations are well-kept secrets. Espionage was an invisible cloak that the recruits had to learn to slip into. Bedi's first trainer was a veteran of cross-border infiltrations, on loan from the IB, who had experience in all things Pakistan. To the trainer's delight, Bedi spoke more than passable Urdu and was well-versed in the customs and traditions of Islam, thanks to his many Muslim friends and his tendency to pick up details. He could also write the Urdu alphabet. The only thing Bedi took some time to master was spy parlance. A 'dead drop' was a coordinated handoff in which a source would leave a physical object—data, cash, weapons parts—in an agreed-upon hiding spot; 'dry cleaning' was a counter-surveillance technique; a 'legend' was their false but credible identity; and a 'cobbler' was the one who would create this identity with fake passports and documents.

'"Uncle"?' Bedi exclaimed while memorising the language of espionage. 'What kind of code is that?'

'"Uncle" is the Intelligence code for headquarters,' his trainer replied. 'Do not look so shocked. Spies can also be funny sometimes!'

Within a week, Bedi had learned how to offer namaaz. In a month, he could pepper his conversations with references from the Quran. The trainer decided not to waste any more time and passed him on for further training to Sankaran Nair.

While Bedi had been immersed in his initial training, Nair had embarked on a secret mission of his own. He made a short trip to France, ostensibly on an official visit. In fact, he had gone to meet a mole, a double agent, whom he had helped to infiltrate the Pakistan government during his stint with IB's West Pakistan desk. The mole was one of Nair's most valuable assets. Nair would meet up with his mole sporadically in various European countries which were considered safe. However, even then, Nair and the agent made sure to cover up all trails when they travelled. The meetings were always short, and the venues were always public places where messages would be left behind at pre-decided dead drops. It was at one of these meetings that the mole had confirmed to Nair that the rumours about the growing unrest in East Pakistan were true. When Nair conveyed this information to Kao, the chief decided it was time for mass training and spy insertions into the country. Kashmir Bedi and other handpicked men would receive advanced training from R&AW agents primed by Nair.

'Welcome and relax,' the agent handler said during the first session. 'Espionage is all about gathering information for your government and not getting caught while doing it.' The handlers were encouraged to interact with new recruits; it was imperative for them to develop a close relationship with their agents, help shape their enthusiasm and take care of their mental well-being.

The training programme was short and to the point. Bedi and his fellow recruits were trained in the art of being present yet absent in a way that no one would notice them in the foreign country. Most importantly, the new recruits were coached on how to identify spies from the enemy camp. They were taught some common characteristics to look out for. Among other things, they were taught to watch out for men and women who would take an extra interest in everything, go to office even on holidays, and work extra hours.

It was hammered into them, 'You shall never use these tricks in pursuance of your personal needs. These methods are meant solely to be employed in the service of the nation.'

Bedi's primary mission was reconnaissance. Everything else would be an added advantage. R&AW needed Intelligence on vital installations in Pakistan and Bedi had been trained to use a camera as well as identify targets without being too obtrusive. After receiving his basic training in photography, he was asked to click stealth photos of the Jalandhar Cantonment without getting caught. When he showed his photos to his coach, the latter chided him. 'There will always be opportunities, Bedi. For instance, look at those two kids there—perfectly normal for a tourist to take a cute picture of two little boys playing. But if you'd aimed for it, you'd have got a better angle of this building, which you have only half-captured. You don't need to get me a beautiful shot with the perfect composition. You only needed to capture the entry–exit points. You are going back next week.'

Bedi had also been given basic hand-to-hand combat training to get out of sticky situations. Apart from teaching them self-protection skills, combat training of recruits also instilled confidence in them, killing the fear that stems from one's innate instinct for self-preservation. Needless to say, a person feels better equipped to take on dangerous tasks if they have been trained to take care of themselves.

While Bedi and the others were training to be spies, Kao had been busy setting up another department— the Photo Interpretation Department. Back in those days, the ARC had powerful aerial cameras mounted on their planes which could click lateral photographs, capturing images up to seventy kilometres inside Pakistan while still flying within Indian territory. Identifying targets in such a large swathe of landscape required special skills, which the new department would cultivate. These were significant advancements in the field of electronic intelligence or ELINT.

The Photo Interpretation Department would also be involved in making sense of the photos brought in by field agents. It employed agents who could scan the photographs to identify and track targets vis-à-vis the landscape. Today, this task is performed by computers and software, but back in the day, it was still a job that required intensive human labour.

The ideas, technology and operations were now all in place. It was time for the agency to enter the outside world through their freshly trained agents. It was time for the test run.

◻

After three months of training, Kashmir Bedi was finally deemed ready. He was all set to make his way across the border into Pakistan. Naturally, he was nervous, but also raring to go. He had already told his family that he had got a job with the Indian Army, which would require him to travel a lot. Kao assured him that he would be paid a salary of Rs 480 every month and a daily allowance of Rs 150 every time he went to Pakistan, and that his family would be taken care of in his absence.

Bedi had adopted a Muslim identity—Mohammed Ibrahim. He had been given an imported mini

22 mm-reel camera and had been told that while his primary mission objective was surveillance, any scrap of information he could bring back would be more than welcome. There were a number of local army units close to the border on the Pakistani side, and he would also have to report on the nature of the work performed by these units.

The insertion plan was put into motion. Two West Pakistani residents had agreed to meet Bedi at the border and smuggle him across. Army Intelligence officers would escort him till Dera Baba Nanak in Gurdaspur district, where he would have to cross over into Pakistan. There was only one thing left to do.

'Are you sure about this?' Bedi's handler asked him before he was wheeled into the operating room.

'I am, sir,' was all he said.

Bedi's circumcision was a short procedure, performed without any complications.

□

Kashmir Bedi entered West Pakistan just before dawn. They knew it would be the best time to cross over as barely any Pakistani ranger patrols were active at this time of day.

Kao was running the entire insertion operation from R&AW headquarters, only recently moved to its new office on Lodhi Road in Delhi. He had worked out a system of communication. The officers escorting Bedi would call in the developments by radio, on a dedicated frequency, to a house in Amritsar. From there, a secure telephone line would communicate the information to a residential house in Delhi. A messenger from the house would then rush on a motorbike to a public telephone, using which he would relay the information to Kao's team at Lodhi Road.

Dawn was breaking over the horizon when the phone rang again in the small room at R&AW headquarters where three men had waited all night. The man at the desk snatched the receiver off its cradle and snapped a 'Yes' into the mouthpiece. Then he listened wordlessly for half a minute before hanging up without saying a word. When he turned around to meet Kao's eyes, he was smiling.

Kashmir Bedi had been successfully inserted into Pakistan.

Over the coming months, countless agents like Bedi were trained, given new identities and inserted into West Pakistan, East Pakistan, Sri Lanka and other neighbouring countries. Most of these spies operated independently, especially in Pakistan, and were ignorant of each other's identities. This secrecy was paramount. In the event of the arrest of one spy, the network had to remain protected. Every month, R&AW inserted a new batch of spies, as the ones who had been on the ground for a while were likelier to get caught by Pakistan's counter-intelligence.

The information gathered over time proved to be invaluable. Bedi and other spies continued to move back and forth across the border, carrying priceless insights and a wealth of photographs. One day, at R&AW's Photo Interpretation Department, personnel scanning the photos that Indian spies had brought back from their latest trip were shocked by what they saw. Some brand new American-made APCs were being unloaded from a cargo plane at one of Pakistan's airbases. The planes were ferrying men and artillery. The agent who detected this rushed to Kao with the pictures. Kao immediately took the new information to Indira Gandhi.

The pictures only confirmed what Kao and Gandhi had been suspecting for some time. The US had violated their arms embargo and were secretly supplying weapons to Pakistan, their NATO ally. In 1965, President Lyndon Johnson had imposed an arms embargo on India and Pakistan, suspending sales of arms to both countries. Five years later, the US— under President Richard Nixon—violated the arms embargo. The US chose to call it an exception, but this 'exception' included six F-104 fighter planes, seven B-57 bombers and three hundred armoured personnel carriers. And this aid to Pakistan confirmed that the latter was preparing for something big.

Kao and Gandhi knew that the time was ripe for an intervention. India needed to prepare to take on West Pakistan even as the situation in East Pakistan was deteriorating by the day.

Chapter 5

Rebellion

LANGUAGE, FOR MILLENNIA, HAS FACILITATED THE exchange of information and growth of civilisations. Throughout human history, words have helped spread ideas, knowledge, scientific inventions and discoveries. It has also been the carrier of cultural phenomena. Hence, the development of language is believed to be the single-most significant event in human evolution. Language is also an important element of identity—of individuals as well as society. It was the struggle to preserve their linguistic and cultural identity that led the people of East Pakistan to rise in revolt against West Pakistan.

On 14 August 1947, Pakistan had declared its independence as a nation, which included the territory of East Bengal (rechristened as East Pakistan). Muhammad Ali Jinnah took up the reins of the new country. But the young nation's joy was short-lived as cracks started to appear in its edifice, owing largely to a deepening rift between East and West Pakistanis.

In his book *Shame*, Salman Rushdie described Pakistan as 'that fantastic bird of a place, two Wings without a body, sundered by the landmass of its greatest foe, joined by nothing but God.'[3] Small wonder, then, that the two parts of Pakistan grappled in vain with the task of finding a common identity. In the east, Bengali Muslims were struggling to identify with a Pakistani national identity purely on the basis of a shared religion. However, differences in ideology, customs and language had already created a deep chasm which would never be bridged.

In February 1948, the Government of Pakistan declared Urdu as the official national language and the people of East Pakistan rose in revolt. Their language was Bangla, they asserted, and so it would remain. Even then, few could have imagined that the nudge towards using language as a tool to unify a geographically separated country would divide it even further.

The Pakistani rulers failed to understand this innate dissimilarity and kept working towards building a cultural bridge. They thought that by making Urdu the common language, they would bring the country together. Prompted by this misguided and myopic vision, they persisted in pushing Urdu as the sole official language and were surprised when their unifying strategy immediately backfired.

---

[3] Salman Rushdie, *Shame* (Macmillan Education, UK, 1983), p. 178.

The first protest against the Pakistan government's diktat broke out at Dhaka University on 11 March 1948. Sheikh Mujibur Rahman, a university student at the time, was amongst the key participants. What might have been a one-off incident escalated when the police fired at the protesting students. Thus began East Bengal's long fight to assert their distinct identity.

The situation worsened when Jinnah visited Dhaka on 21 March 1948, to declare 'Urdu and only Urdu as the sole language.'[4] Following these two incidents, East Pakistan witnessed numerous rallies and protests. The Bhasha Andolan, or fight to preserve the 'right to language', soon turned into a mass rebellion, an assertion of East Pakistan's Bengali cultural identity.

The rebellion gave birth to the country's first opposition party: the Awami Muslim League. Maulana Abdul Khan Hamid Bhashani, an Islamic scholar and a political leader, was the first president of the party.

The Awami Muslim League's manifesto contained forty-two crucial points, the most important of which was the recognition of Bengali as a state language. The manifesto proved to be a major impetus to the Bhasha Andolan. Sheikh Mujibur Rahman was actively involved in framing the demands and agendas of the

---

[4] Sanghamitra Mazumdar, 'International Mother Language Day, Ekushe February, Bangla and History of Bhasha Dibas', *The Statesman*, 20 February 2019.

League, which soon dropped the word 'Muslim' from its name as a mark of its secularism. Rahman went on to serve as commerce minister of East Pakistan after the 1954 general elections, in which the League formed a coalition with three other parties.

Rahman's ascent to power began in March 1957 when Maulana Bhashani resigned from his post as president of the Awami League. Rahman stepped in and took over the reins of the party. Around the same time, in West Pakistan, General Ayub Khan grabbed power by means of a military coup. Khan's regime pushed East and West Pakistan further apart; Rahman and the general remained at loggerheads throughout the latter's tenure as president.

In 1962, Ayub Khan drafted a new constitution which concentrated all the executive powers in the hands of the president—the president of Pakistan no longer needed the approval of its legislature. Khan ushered in a 'great decade' for West Pakistan with his advocacy of capitalist industrialisation for uplifting the impoverished nation. However, during this 'decade of progress' for the West Pakistanis, their eastern counterparts were entirely ignored. They continued to struggle with abysmal standards of living and widespread poverty. Even the money earned in East Pakistan was used to develop its western territories. The centralised government systematically enforced the economic and political subordination of its East Bengali citizens.

The 1965 Indo-Pakistan war served to accentuate Ayub Khan's atrocious policies of discrimination. East Pakistan was completely cut off during the war. It had only one infantry division of its own, a single battalion of fighters and no navy. Had it been attacked by India, East Pakistan would have been extremely vulnerable—in other words, incapable of defending itself.

In short, after the war, East Pakistan was smarting at being treated like the poor cousin of West Pakistan. Rahman harnessed the energy of the politically discontented and economically frustrated East Bengalis, igniting a nationalist explosion. He believed that it was now more important than ever for East Pakistan to be self-sufficient in all respects.

In 1966, Rehman published a booklet outlining his six-point movement for East Pakistani autonomy. It demanded the following:

1. The constitution should ensure the supremacy of the legislature by upholding direct democracy.
2. The responsibilities of the federal government should be limited to defence and foreign affairs.
3. Two separate and freely convertible currencies should be introduced, and an independent banking reserve should be established.

4. Federal units should have the power of taxation and revenue collection.

5. There should be two separate accounts for the foreign exchange earnings of the two regions, and they should be encouraged to establish trade links with foreign countries independently.

6. Lastly, East Pakistan should have a separate militia or paramilitary force.

The leaders of West Pakistan perceived Rahman's six-point programme as a device to dissect Pakistan. They not only rejected his proposal outright but also projected him as a separatist.

While the Pakistan government was trying to portray Mujibur Rahman as an anti-nationalist in the east, Ayub Khan's own foreign minister, Zulfikar Ali Bhutto, resigned from his post and founded the Pakistan People's Party in 1967, creating a socialist opposition in the west.

It was at this juncture that the Awami League got in touch with the IB in India. The R&AW hadn't been formed yet.

❏

At the time, Sankaran Nair was handling the Pakistan desk at IB. His subordinate, P.N. Ojha, was posted in Dhaka and had been liaising with a network of political activists of the Awami League, navy employees and

police officers in East Pakistan. Nair had received news
through his mole that West Pakistan had been planning
action against the East Bengalis. When members of
the Awami League reached out to Nair via Ojha, he
decided to set up a meeting with them. Under the alias
of Colonel Menon, Nair himself met up with some of
these officers and agents on the India–Pakistan border
near Agartala.

These men suspected that West Pakistan was
planning an offensive against East Pakistan and were
seeking help in the form of an arms supply from
India. They wanted to begin an armed uprising in East
Pakistan against their central government.

Nair promised them that the IB would send arms
for an insurgency but advised them not to jump the
gun; they needed to plan thoroughly for the revolt,
he said. The weapons would be dispatched on a barge
down the Meghna River from Agartala and they could
collect the cargo at suitable destinations.

Before the mutiny could gain momentum,
however, the governor of East Pakistan, Abdul Monem
Khan, unearthed the plan. He convinced Ayub Khan
that the 'Agartala Conspiracy' would be the perfect
opportunity to implicate Mujibur Rahman and quell
his rising popularity in East Pakistan.

Ayub Khan's government charged Rahman with
sedition for his alleged collaboration with India to

bring about the secession of East Pakistan. Along with Rahman, hundreds of other East Bengalis were charged by the authorities with incitement and treason for plotting to bring about the partition of East and West Pakistan. But it soon became evident that Pakistani military intelligence was unable to prove a single case against any of them. Despite this failure, Rahman was detained in custody for three years.

Ayub Khan had hoped to discredit Rahman and the Awami League by branding them as traitors. Instead, this turn of events only increased Rahman's popularity and that of his six-point movement. The East Bengalis now saw Rahman as a true patriot who was fighting for their collective independence.

Rahman and other members of the Awami League were finally absolved of all charges and freed on 22 February 1969.

As Rahman became the rising star in the east, Ayub Khan's sun was setting in the west. He was facing criticism from all fronts in his country. His envisioned development policies had failed in every sector, and his falling out with Zulfikar Ali Bhutto had created a formidable political rival. Bhutto's popularity was on the rise, and he was looking to topple Khan's government. In the east, the Agartala Conspiracy case and the Bhasha Andolan were brewing an atmosphere of strife. Rahman had already drawn the battle lines for the autonomy of East Pakistan. The people of Pakistan were generally dissatisfied with Ayub Khan's long and rather uneventful rule. In a nutshell, Khan was besieged by civilian discontent and political opposition all around the country. Riots were causing perpetual unrest across East and West Pakistan.

Finally, on 25 March 1969, Ayub Khan handed over the presidency of Pakistan to General Yahya Khan in a peaceful coup. Indira Gandhi immediately called for a meeting with her close confidants and policymakers to take stock of the changing scenario in the subcontinent. She wanted to understand how Yahya Khan's regime could change India's position and actions.

'Yahya is a big drunkard,' Kao said, 'but he is close to the Americans, and this is the real worry.'

Yahya Khan tried to bridge the vast chasm between the two regions of Pakistan when he took over the presidency. He began by imposing martial law and abrogating the 1962 constitution. However, he also realised that some concessions had to be made to the autonomists of East Pakistan if the thin fabric of Pakistani unity was to be maintained.

In March 1970, President Yahya Khan announced a Legal Framework Order, calling for direct elections to a unicameral legislature. It was to secure the future constitution which would be written after the polls, one that would safeguard Pakistan's territorial integrity and Islamic ideology. He ended the equal distribution of seats between East and West Pakistan and promised fair and direct 'one man, one vote' elections. He thus addressed the chief grievances of the East Pakistanis and took his first steps to start over.

The national election was to be held in October 1970, and it was East Pakistan's only hope. In a historic speech on 28 October 1970, relayed on Radio Pakistan, Rahman voiced his vision for the imminent elections. He addressed East Pakistan as Bengal—at the time, the word 'Bengal' was forbidden on Pakistani radio and television. He outlined his vision for a new country that was based on the principles of equality and democracy, one that would be free from hunger and poverty. He declared that, on being elected to power, he would make the sectors of agriculture, education and health his top priorities.

East Pakistanis showered Rahman with fervent devotion. Their 'Bangabandhu', friend of Bengal, was here.

□

From the shadows, Kao watched Rahman's meteoric rise to power, aware that a world leader was emerging in East Pakistan. Ever since the formation of R&AW in 1968, Indian operatives had been in contact with the pro-Rahman faction. It was through P.N. Banerjee that Kao and R&AW had gained direct access to Rahman and other Awami League leaders in East Pakistan.

The leadership in East Pakistan was irked by the constant discrimination that they were facing from the ruling government, and were more than willing to help and receive help from India. Banerjee was on-ground, making friends with the faction. He worked covertly from R&AW's office in Calcutta. Gradually, he approached Rahman through common friends. His methods were slow and deliberate, building trust. He knew that it was important to establish a long-term relationship between India and East Pakistan, and that Rahman was vital for this alliance.

They had connected quite easily. Speaking the same language had bridged the gap of nationality. Both Banerjee and Rahman were aware of the political value their association carried. But eventually, they forged a deep bond of friendship that went beyond politics.

The same reason that had instigated the war-cry in the region had joined their leader to an organisation which could help them overthrow their suppressors.

With the election approaching, Zulfikar Ali Bhutto launched a full-fledged campaign. But while Rahman had the foresight to put up a few candidates in West Pakistan, Bhutto foolishly completely ignored East Pakistan.

Even as Kao and Sankaran Nair were plotting their next move to deal with Pakistan, Mother Nature interfered with everyone's plans. Literally and metaphorically, a storm was brewing in East Pakistan. Cyclone Bhola is still counted among the world's deadliest tropical storms.

It hit East Pakistan on 12 November 1970, sweeping a quarter of a million people, with their animals, crops, houses and livelihoods, into the Bay of Bengal. An estimated 4.8 million people were affected by the cyclone. It was a heart-wrenching scene; East Bengal was facing significant destruction.

The elections were postponed to December because of the cyclone. If there was one chance for the Yahya Khan regime to redeem itself in the eyes of East Pakistanis, it was this horrific tragedy. However, for reasons best known to him, the president took almost a week to even respond to the disaster. And then, surveying the damage from the air while returning from a successful trip to China, a hungover Yahya Khan is reported to have said, 'It does not look that bad after all.'[5]

India offered to lend its aircraft for relief operations, but the offer was declined for political reasons.

---

[5] Naomi Hossain, 'The 1970 Bhola Cyclone, Nationalist Politics and the Subsistence Crisis Contract in Bangladesh', *Disasters*: https://onlinelibrary.wiley.com/doi/10.1111/disa.12235, 28 April, 2017, p. 8.

Meanwhile, the Awami League's ailing Maulana Bhashani made an exhausting journey to the cyclone-affected areas of East Bengal. Even though he was extremely unwell, he met victims of the disaster and engaged in relief work. He later told the press what the people had told him: '*Ora keu ashe ni* (None of them came).'[6] West Pakistan had not deemed the destruction severe enough to offer any aid.

Maulana Bhashani returned to Dhaka and staged a mass event at Paltan Maidan, where he expressed his anger against the Government of Pakistan for their indifference to citizens affected by the cyclone in the east. He called the leaders out for their apathy and arrogance. He ended his speech with the fiery slogan, 'East Pakistan Zindabad.'[7] His anger and clarity struck a chord with the people. Three days later, Mujibur Rahman followed with a rousing call of his own: 'East Pakistan must achieve self-rule by ballot if possible, and by bullet, if necessary.'[8]

Rahman then led the livid, helpless East Pakistanis into a political uprising against the Centre. He declared that the failure to respond to the cyclone efficiently was a failure of the Pakistani state, not merely of the Yahya Khan regime.

---

[6] Ibid, p. 9.

[7] Ibid, p. 8.

[8] David Ludden, 'The Politics of Independence of Bangladesh', *Economic & Political Weekly*, 27 August 2011, Vol. 46, Issue no. 35, pp. 79–85.

Yahya Khan later apologised publicly for his failure to act in the face of immense international pressure, especially from the US. But the damage had already been done.

❑

R&AW, meanwhile, assessed the growing unrest and sensed the possibility of Pakistan resorting to war with India. Shortly after the cyclone, R&AW submitted another report to the prime minister, which spelt out the need for 'surgical intervention'.

These reports were followed by the information that Richard Nixon had started selling weapons to Pakistan. Yahya Khan was being rewarded for the anti-communist and pro-US stance he had adopted after Nixon was turned away by India during the Cold War. Together, the two countries had made it their business to create as many problems as they could for India. In Punjab, they encouraged the Sikhs in a separatist movement which demanded an independent state by the name of Khalistan. They planned to assist in the destabilisation of Punjab.

While India was preparing for the worst, elections were conducted in Pakistan on 7 December 1970. R&AW had known that Mujibur Rahman would win by a landslide and were not surprised by the results at all: Rahman and the Awami League emerged victorious with an absolute majority in both East and West Pakistan. It now remained to be seen whether Yahya Khan would draw up a new constitution with the Awami League. Kao, Haksar and Indira Gandhi were well aware that Rahman's victory would not go down well with either Yahya Khan or Zulfikar Ali Bhutto. And this would only lead to more friction between East and West Pakistan.

Chapter 6

Skyjack

TWO YOUNG MEN WERE QUIETLY RECITING A VERSE from the Quran. In their late teens, they had freshly sprouted moustaches. They finished their prayers and looked at each other. Their sweaty palms were clenched in their trouser pockets. One man signalled to the other with a nod.

In swift, synchronised movements, they got up, pulled weapons out of their bags and shouted, 'THIS PLANE IS HIJACKED!'

The passengers on the flight started screaming. It was an Air India plane. The year was 1971.

An hour back, on that cold winter morning in January, when the two men with handguns had entered the Srinagar airport, they were able to make their way to the boarding gate with relative ease. In 1971, air travel was a luxury; only a few people could afford it. The airports were relatively empty and airport security was not very strict.

Passengers had lined up in a small queue to enter the flight, which was scheduled to take off in half an hour for Jammu. The men were nervous, and one of them even stammered a little when he was asked his name at the security check. However, they were barely given a second glance by the officer on duty. Their identity documents and tickets were checked, and then the two men walked right up the stairs attached to the aircraft, a Fokker Friendship F-27. It was called Ganga.

The two men kept glancing over their shoulders apprehensively, almost as if they were expecting to be stopped or have their names called out. But they boarded the aircraft without incident and took their seats. The men had butterflies in their stomachs. There were two reasons for this: it was the first time they were travelling on an aeroplane, and they were going to hijack the flight.

They fastened their seat belts and sat quietly in their seats, their bodies stiff with tension. The plane taxied on the runway and gently rose into the air. Steadily, it gained altitude and then straightened, settling into its flight path for Jammu.

The man at the window, Hashim Qureshi, looked at his companion and cousin, Ashraf Qureshi. They nodded to each other. '*La ilaha illallah. Mohammad ul rasoolallah,*' they both whispered.

They unfastened their seat belts, bent down and pulled a gun and a hand grenade out of their bags. For a moment, they looked into each other's eyes, as if gathering courage. Then they put their plan into motion. Hashim rushed into the cockpit with his gun, while Ashraf stood outside the cockpit door, holding up his hand grenade. The passengers broke out into screams and sobs. Ashraf, nervous himself, yelled at the passengers to remain calm. They were stunned into silence.

◻

The dramatic events of that afternoon had their genesis in Pakistan's December 1970 general elections. Mujibur Rahman's resounding victory had astonished and humiliated the ruling West Pakistan government. They had always considered the East Pakistanis to be inferior to them and had never imagined that the day would come when a Bengali Muslim would be able to form a government in West Pakistan. The impossible, nevertheless, had happened. Rahman had managed to win 161 seats in a 300-member parliament.

Consequently, Yahya Khan delayed the formation of the government indefinitely. This blatant snub of the popular mandate was widely condemned in East Pakistan. Rahman used this opportunity to raise the cry for complete independence from Pakistan, and the entire population of the erstwhile East Bengal stood behind him. Mass protests were organised across the whole region.

To manage the ongoing crisis and buy some time, Bhutto started engaging Mujibur Rahman in talks. At the same time, Yahya Khan started playing another dangerous game. He began ferrying men, material and army personnel from West Pakistan to East Pakistan. The families of officers posted in East Pakistan were also called back.

At R&AW's Lodhi Road headquarters, Kao and Nair were monitoring the developments in Pakistan closely. The coup, Ayub Khan's defeat, Yahya Khan's ascension to power, Sheikh Mujibur Rahman's victory, and the ongoing negotiations for power, were all being documented and analysed by Kao and his team. Kao was also getting rather worried about the increasingly frequent flights between West and East Pakistan. Yahya Khan maintained that the flights were part of the ongoing talks between Bhutto and Rahman. However, the on-ground R&AW agents in West and East Pakistan had conveyed their suspicions that a bigger plan was afoot.

Pakistan's political geography was absurd; East Pakistan was more than two thousand kilometres away from its western counterpart. All planes flying from West Pakistan to East Pakistan flew over India, as it was the shortest route available. If R&AW could find a plausible reason to get those overflights to stop, they might also be able to foil the grand plot that Yahya Khan had in mind.

In the same week that Kao and Nair had realised that they needed a strong reason to stop the movement of Pakistani aircraft through Indian airspace, a report had landed on Kao's desk. It was one among many that were routinely sent by various agencies to R&AW as part of standard procedure. The Border Security Force (BSF), when it had sent the report, had no way of knowing what the information it contained was going to be of worth.

The report mentioned a man named Hashim Qureshi, who had been arrested at the Indo-Pak border for trying to smuggle arms and explosives into the country. He was quickly overpowered by BSF guards, packed into a vehicle and driven to the nearest interrogation centre.

After making him sweat alone for an hour, two veteran BSF officers entered the interrogation room. Hashim, a scared seventeen-year-old, was more than willing to talk. He was a young foot-soldier who had been motivated by lofty ideals to sign up for a bigger cause—to free the Kashmir that he loved. He firmly believed that Kashmir was the one and only cause worth fighting for.

Slowly, and in great detail, Hashim described how he had visited Peshawar in 1969 to spend a few days with his uncle. There, he had been introduced to Maqbool Bhat, the founder of the National Liberation Front (NLF), which would go on to become the infamous Jammu and Kashmir Liberation Front. The young and impressionable Hashim was quickly brainwashed and recruited for the Kashmir cause. He was trained in the use of guns and bombs at one of the many camps run by the NLF.

Hashim was then assigned to an important mission—hijacking an Indian commercial aircraft— which the NLF would use as leverage to push its agenda. Hashim told the officers that he was even taken to Chaklala airport in Rawalpindi to look at an old Fokker Friendship aircraft that was parked there. On his return to Lahore, he was supplied with arms and ammunition, and was told to sneak back into India to execute the hijack plan. It was on his way back into India that he had been arrested.

The demands NLF planned to make had been simple. They wanted thirty-six members who were serving time in Indian prisons to be freed, besides drawing attention to their cause.

'NLF was going to liberate Kashmir with one hijacked aircraft?' one of the BSF interrogators asked quizzically.

'I was to hijack the aircraft which would be piloted by Rajiv Gandhi,' Hashim revealed, and added, 'I was not the only one, sir. There were others as well.'

The BSF officers looked at each other in shock.

❑

As Kao sat in his office, scrutinising the report sent by the BSF, the wheels were already turning in his head. During his interrogation, Hashim had described the hijack plan as well as the basic training that he had received at the NLF camp down to the last detail. He had begged the BSF authorities for clemency and agreed to cooperate wholeheartedly.

After going over the report thoroughly, Kao formulated a plan. Hashim could prove to be the solution they needed.

One would never know what happened behind closed doors, but the BSF convinced Hashim that hijacking a flight called Ganga would be beneficial to them both. The success of the mission would anoint Hashim as a hero in the eyes of the NLF, and it would prove to be a worthy impetus to the Kashmir cause. And the BSF, too, would get what they desired. Hashim couldn't believe his luck. It was a win-win situation for him. The BSF told him that he would get access to the aircraft but he would have to plan and execute the hijack himself.

As part of the deal, Hashim was made an honorary member of the BSF. He was also given an appointment letter announcing that he was now a member of the Bangalore Battalion 102. A mere teenager, Hashim was overjoyed to receive a reward instead of a punishment, considering the circumstances.

Hashim started his job and performed it diligently. He was to be on duty at the Srinagar airport for several days, keeping a watch on the people who entered and exited it. He was given complete access to the airport and ample opportunity to familiarise himself with its layout. After a few weeks, he knew that it was time for him to keep up his end of the bargain. Hashim was ready to hijack a plane.

However, he would need an accomplice. He reached out to his young cousin, Ashraf Qureshi. Ashraf was close to him in age and someone whom Hashim knew he could trust. Soon, Ashraf joined him in Srinagar. Hashim told him about the plan and convinced him of the glory it would bring to the NLF. They began to plan the hijack. The Qureshis intended to force the plane to land in Rawalpindi. The passengers would be their leverage to fulfil the demands of the NLF. They knew they would need weapons to induce fear and submission on-board the flight. An advertisement had appeared in a newspaper of a real-looking pistol which could be used to scare thieves away. Hashim ordered one by post. Ashraf fabricated a wooden hand grenade and painted it a metallic colour.

On 30 January 1971, the Qureshis put their plan into action. The plane they would be hijacking, the Ganga, was actually a tired old thing, acquired by the Indian Airlines after it had been decommissioned by the Indian Army.

◻

News of the hijacking—broadcast nationwide by the All India Radio—caused a sensation across the country. Aboard the Ganga, everything went smoothly until they faced their first hiccup mid-air.

The plane had changed course and was on its way to Rawalpindi when Captain M.K. Kachru, who was piloting the aircraft, announced to the Qureshis that Ganga did not have enough fuel to make it to their destination. They would have to land in Lahore instead.

The duo was not happy with this unforeseen change of plans, but they knew they would have to improvise and manage somehow. As long as they had the passengers, they told themselves, their demands would be met.

The personnel at the Lahore Air Traffic Control Centre had heard of the hijacking on the news and were still trying to make sense of it when Captain Kachru's voice crackled on the radio, requesting immediate permission to land. It wasn't a quick decision, or an easy one, but Yahya Khan's office finally consented to the landing. If the plane ran out of fuel while in Pakistani airspace and crashed on Pakistani soil, it would become an international incident.

Mysteriously, a small group of mediapersons were already at the Lahore airport by the time Ganga touched down on the runway and made its way to a secluded corner chalked out for it. The journalists rushed forward with their cameras and voice recorders, surrounding the plane as it came to a halt. No amount of threatening or pleading by security forces could induce them to back off. Even as the Pakistani Army rushed to the scene to secure the airport, the door of the aircraft opened and Hashim appeared on the top step.

'We demand the immediate release of thirty-six of our brothers from the NLF, failing which we will kill all these hostages. What the Indian Government does from now on is completely in their hands,'[9] Hashim said before turning and going back into the aircraft.

Back in India, Kao and his team at R&AW, along with the PMO, followed the news of the hijacking.

Meanwhile, Zulfikar Ali Bhutto was in a lunch meeting with Sheikh Mujibur Rahman in Dhaka when

---

[9] Praveen Swami, *India, Pakistan and the Secret Jihad: The Covert War in Kashmir 1947–2004* (Routledge, New York, 2006), p. 113.

news of the hijacking broke. He immediately left for Lahore.

Hijackings were practically unheard of in those days. Hence, the incident aroused considerable curiosity and interest across the globe. The Pakistan government, feeling the eyes of the world on them, knew that they would have to tackle the situation with a great deal of tact.

Bhutto arrived at the Lahore airport, and with a tight security escort, he went up to the hijackers, listened patiently to their demands, and hugged them before leaving. He convinced them to let go of the passengers.

The teenagers did as they were told. The Pakistani authorities extended warm hospitality to the hijackers as well as the passengers. The hostages were put up in five-star hotels in Lahore even as Indian and Pakistani authorities negotiated the demands of the hijackers. Two days later, the passengers returned to India.

Meanwhile, Hashim and Ashraf met up with and were feted by the NLF chief, Maqbool Bhat, at the Lahore airport. It was then decided that the best course of action would be to set the plane on fire. They wanted to send out a strong statement by burning an Indian aircraft.

Hashim and Ashraf set the plane ablaze in full view of the media. But it turned out to be a foolish move.

The hijackers now had no plane and no passengers. The negotiations fell through, and the Qureshis were arrested.

By then, all the former hostages were back in India and safe in their homes. Pakistan was crying itself hoarse, saying that it had had nothing to do with the hijacking. As for Sheikh Mujibur Rahman, he was telling anyone who would listen that this had been engineered by West Pakistan to divert attention from the ongoing crisis in East Pakistan and to delay the transfer of power.

◻

Everyone was wondering what India would do next.

'As you rightly said, madam, we should not believe Pakistan. We should let the investigation run its course before we do anything.' Kao was sitting in the PMO. Across the desk, Indira Gandhi had already started smiling.

'And, till then, what do you suggest, Ramji?' she asked Kao.

'Till then, of course, we cannot allow any overflights through Indian airspace from West Pakistan to East Pakistan,' Kao said, smiling back at Gandhi. 'This is a breach of security for India.'

After the hijack, there were some reports in the Pakistani newspapers that Hashim had been recruited by Kao and R&AW to aid them in the war against Pakistan. There was no concrete proof to this effect, but one thing is certain: Hashim's act definitely helped India. Citing security concerns after the hijack, India banned Pakistani flights from using Indian airspace. This restricted Pakistan's movements and considerably increased flying time between West and East Pakistan. Earlier, planes from West Pakistan could fly directly over India to land at Dhaka in three to four hours. Now Pakistani planes would have to circumnavigate India to land at Colombo, Sri Lanka, refuel, and then move on to East Pakistan. It was a much longer, more expensive journey.

And Yahya Khan was not happy with this turn of events.

Chapter 7

A Bloodbath

'It's confirmed,' one of the on-ground operatives in West Pakistan told a senior R&AW agent in a covert meeting. 'I spoke to one of our guys who works at the Karachi airport. Three large government convoys entered the airport last week.' There was an escalation of activity and R&AW had been receiving confirmations from multiple sources that they had set up in Pakistan—a loader working at the airport, a peanut seller hawking his wares at a traffic signal minutes away from the airport, a newspaper vendor with a stall near the Rawalpindi Cantonment—who had seen a plane passing overhead and landing inside. Every input checked out. Now using Colombo as a transit point, people were being transported to West Pakistan from the East, the Bengali army was being moved back to East Pakistan from the West and Bhutto too kept moving between the two regions. Yahya Khan was constantly meeting senior Army officers at the Cantonment.

With each confirmation, the realisation grew stronger. A massive outcome was imminent.

The next input came from Sri Lanka. When R&AW had started developing their network of foot soldiers, they had inserted field agents into Sri Lanka as well. Hundreds of Tamil-speaking men were screened, recruited and trained to be placed into the country, where Tamil was the second language. Kao had already started reaping the benefits of having placed his agents in various menial jobs in Pakistan, and the same strategy was used in Sri Lanka as well.

It finally paid off when, even as inputs were coming in from Pakistan, Indian undercover operatives in Sri Lanka reported the same observation to their handlers: an unusual number of Pakistan International Airlines flights were stopping to refuel at Colombo before proceeding to Dhaka.

'They don't know what's happening, sir,' one of the handlers told his superior officer, speaking on a payphone miles away from the airport, 'but the number of flights seems to be increasing.'

'Oh, bloody hell!' Sankaran Nair said when he read the reports. 'They're moving the army through commercial flights!'

The writing was on the wall. Yahya Khan was moving in for the kill. And if that was true, there was one thing he would certainly do before he did anything else—take Sheikh Mujibur Rahman out of the picture.

◻

On 3 March 1971, a message found its way to Calcutta from Dhaka. An R&AW operative posted in East Pakistan confirmed Kao's worst suspicions. A radical clampdown was being planned in Dhaka. The message also contained a word of caution: '... advise Menon ... to bring in ... our friends.'[10]

Menon was Col. Menon, Sankaran Nair's alias, and 'our friends' referred to Mujibur Rahman and the leaders of the Awami League.

Kao, when he received the report, looked pensive. Averting the war in East Pakistan was no longer a possibility. He knew that Rahman had to be secured, and instructed Banerjee to reach out to Bangabandhu immediately to warn him. Banerjee left at once for Dhaka to alert Rahman and the Awami League.

In West Pakistan, the seeds of the plan to capture Mujibur Rahman had been sown three months earlier. In December 1970, Yahya Khan and Bhutto, still smarting from the shock of Rahman's victory in the elections, had asked him to reconsider the results of the vote. However, Rahman was adamant that Yahya Khan keep his promise and hand over the reins of power.

---

[10] Asoka Raina, *Inside R&AW* (Vikas Publishing House, New Delhi, 1982), pp. 48, 49, 50.

Yahya, of course, had no such intention. Unable to convince Rahman to back off, he decided to bring him down.

It was in Larkana, the hometown of Zulfikar Ali Bhutto, that the plot of the genocide in East Pakistan was conceived. After the elections, a furious Yahya Khan and Bhutto went on a duck-shooting trip to Larkana. There, between the sounds of gunshots, the Larkana conspiracy was hatched. It was a cruel, comprehensive and final plan to crush the resistance in the east and dismember the region once and for all. It aimed at depriving East Pakistan of a successor government and abandoning it to anarchy, so that West Pakistan could swoop in and take over.

Step by step, the plan was implemented. Khan and Bhutto began by postponing the National Assembly that was to be held on 1 February 1971, a move that they knew would spur Rahman into action. Rahman responded by calling for a strike in Dhaka the next day, which swiftly spread all over East Pakistan.

Then Yahya Khan waited for a month before announcing that the Assembly would be held on 6 March 1971. Simultaneously, he appointed Tikka Khan as governor and martial law administrator of East Pakistan.

Fed up with Yahya Khan's empty promises, Rahman established a provisional government in East Pakistan on 8 March. He declared, 'Build forts in each homestead. You must resist the Pakistani enemy with whatever you have in hand. Remember, we have given a lot of blood, a lot more blood we shall give if need be, but we shall liberate the people of this country, Insha Allah. The struggle this time is the struggle for our emancipation; the struggle this time is the struggle for independence. Joy Bangla!'[11]

As part of the struggle for complete independence, Rahman initiated people's rule in East Pakistan. He urged that the martial law be lifted and power be transferred to the elected representatives of the people. He gave directives for a civil disobedience movement to the people of East Pakistan. Black flags were raised on rooftops for a week. Rahman also asked for a total shutdown in the region, striking at the Pakistani economy by stopping all money transfers between east and west for an indefinite period. Even the chief justice of East Pakistan refused to swear Tikka Khan in as governor.

By 24 March 1971, all talks and negotiations for a united Pakistan between Yahya Khan, Bhutto and Rahman had failed. Rahman had stuck to his guns, and on 25 March, he made a formal and public demand for a separate nation. This would be a nation for the Bengalis by the Bengalis, known as Bangladesh.

---

[11] Antara Dutta, *Refugees and Borders in South Asia: The Great Exodus of 1971* (Routledge, New York, 2012), p. 8.

This declaration was the breaking point for Yahya Khan.

Tikka Khan was chosen to spearhead an attack which would break the spirit of the 'lowly Bangalis'.[12] The main target was a no-brainer: it was Bangabandhu, Sheikh Mujibur Rahman himself.

❑

The operation was named Searchlight, and the objective was singular: search and destroy. The operation was to begin once Yahya Khan had safely reached Karachi from Dhaka.

Tikka Khan would in later years be known as the Butcher of Bengal, but he was a terror long before he earned this sinister sobriquet.

Khan had joined the armed forces before Independence, when it was the British Army, and had fought in World War II. After Partition, he opted to go to Pakistan and rose steadily through the ranks until he was posted as a general at the Army General Headquarters in Rawalpindi.

They say that a good soldier commands respect, but a good warrior commands fear. Tikka Khan was known to be ruthless towards his enemies, both on the battlefield and off it. He was revered as a hero in

---

[12] Inam Ahmed and Shakhawat Liton, 'Pakistan Lying, Still: Genocide Plot Conceived at Duck Shooting Trip', *The Daily Star*, 4 December 2015.

Pakistan for his exploits against the Indian Army in the 1965 war. His very presence in East Pakistan was an indication of the fact that Yahya Khan had made up his mind. The movement for freedom was going to be met with swift and brutal action.

Despite knowing this, Rahman refused to leave East Pakistan. 'I will never leave this country,' he told P.N. Banerjee during the urgent personal rendezvous that the latter had requested with the leader.

'We have several reports, sir, that Yahya Khan is coming for you. You must leave; now,' Banerjee pleaded with Rahman.

But Rahman was resolute. He would rather die a hero in his own country than live as a 'coward' in another. A disappointed Banerjee returned to India.

'The man is adamant, Ramji,' Banerjee told Kao, sounding tired. 'He told me that he was perfectly aware that the place was going to burn, and that he was not going to watch it burn from afar.'

'Nath Babu, the idea is that Intelligence can only warn,' Kao told Banerjee. 'The decision to act is always that of the individual.'

Rahman had, however, consented to let R&AW extract his small group of trusted aides from East Pakistan.

R&AW had eyes on Yahya Khan's every move. Reports had started coming in that he was scheduled

to leave Dhaka for Karachi. Time was ticking away for
R&AW. Overnight, plans were drawn up, and R&AW
agents smuggled Mujibur Rahman's closest associates
across the border within a span of hours. The operation
was extremely dangerous, and blood pressures soared
for the entire duration of it. Once everyone was safely
across the border and in West Bengal, Kao and Nair
realised there was only one thing left to do: wait and
watch.

◻

On the night of 25 March 1971, Kao and Nair sat
with a small group of officers in a command centre
that had been set up in the R&AW headquarters on
Lodhi Road. Intelligence reports from the field had
indicated that the operation to crush the resistance
in East Pakistan would begin once Yahya Khan had
reached Karachi. Yahya Khan would not risk being
in East Pakistan or even mid-air when the operation
started.

A final confirmation was received when one of
their agents at the Bandaranaike International Airport
in Colombo reported that Yahya Khan's plane had
stopped to refuel en route from East Pakistan to West
Pakistan. Also on the aircraft were at least two other
VIPs.

Meanwhile, M.B.K. Nair and his team were
continuously monitoring Pakistani radio frequencies

in the command centre set up exclusively to track Operation Searchlight.

Headed by M.B.K. Nair, the still-young agency had successfully set up an intercepting apparatus and established their first satellite communication check-post in Calcutta. Using the device, they were able to tap into Pakistan's west-to-east communication. Thus, R&AW had already begun to master world-class technical Intelligence (TECHINT), the first of its kind.

Of course, using the apparatus wasn't as easy as turning a dial. Pakistan's Inter-Services Intelligence (ISI), fully aware that anyone could be listening to it, would often change frequencies as well as code words. The real challenges were to find the right frequency before some gold nugget of information had slipped away, and to decode the message quickly.

It was through one of these messages intercepted by R&AW that the agency found out that Yahya Khan had safely landed in Karachi on the night of 25 March 1971. It was the confirmation that Tikka Khan was waiting for before he struck. He told his soldiers, 'I want the land and not the people.'[13]

It was a peaceful night in East Pakistan. By dawn, it smelled of blood and fire, the air rent by wails and cries. Gen. Tikka Khan let loose all the terror at his

---

[13] Md Shahnawaz Khan Chandan, 'A History Written in Blood', *The Daily Star*, 16 December 2015.

disposal, as if he were raiding an enemy, not dealing with his own people. The military action was a display of stark cruelty, in many ways more merciless than the massacre at Jallianwala Bagh. The operation had been designed to eliminate all traces of 'trouble-making' elements.

Earlier that night, around 8 p.m., Sheikh Mujibur Rahman had received a secret message through P.N. Banerjee, informing him that his house would be raided at any point by army personnel. Banerjee and Kao had learnt through their sources that a hand grenade was going to be thrown at the car in which Rahman would be taken away, and arrangements had been made to blame Bengali extremists for the act. Following Rahman's death and using it as a pretext, the Pakistani Army would move in and occupy East Pakistan.

Regardless, Rahman decided to remain in his house. He told Banerjee, 'Let them kill me in my own house so that everybody would know that they have killed me, and my blood would purify my people.'[14]

At 10.30 p.m., he called a secret transmitter in Chittagong—the Swadhin Betar Bangla Kendra (Free Bengal Radio). The military had already occupied the Dhaka radio centre, but they hadn't gotten to

---

[14] Sydney H. Schanberg, 'He Tells Full Story of Arrest and Detention', *The New York Times*, 18 January 1972.

Chittagong yet. The Swadhin Betar Bangla Kendra had been defiantly broadcasting in support of the rebels even during the Pakistani clampdown.

Rahman recorded a message asking his people to resist the Pakistani Army and fight on, regardless of what might happen to him. He declared that the 75 million people of East Pakistan were citizens of the sovereign, independent state of Bangladesh.

After recording his message, Rahman dismissed the men of the East Pakistan Rifles, a paramilitary unit that had been guarding him. He also sent away the other politicians of the Awami League who were with him, his eldest son and two daughters. His wife refused to leave, and stayed back with their youngest child. Neither of them realised then that their middle son was still in the house too.

And, within the hour, Dhaka was under attack.

Troops began firing into Rahman's house shortly after midnight. He pushed his wife and children into his dressing room. They got down on the floor as bullets whizzed over their heads.

As the soldiers stormed his home, Rahman came out of the dressing room, his arms raised in the air. He surrendered to the Pakistani Army after saying goodbye to his wife and children. He knew there was a possibility that they would never see each other again.

After midnight, his home telephone went dead.

Kao and his men had gathered at R&AW headquarters that night. They had lost contact with Rahman. Communication with East Pakistan was completely cut off.

The first indication that Operation Searchlight had been a success was the interception of a single radio transmission from Tikka Khan's forces in Dhaka to ISI headquarters in Karachi:

'Big bird is in the cage; others not in the nest. Repeat, big bird is in the cage.'[15]

Banerjee looked at Kao in horror. That could only mean one thing. What they had feared most had come true. The 'big bird' was Rahman, the 'others' alluded to the Awami League, and the 'nest' was East Pakistan.

From his small table in the middle of the room, all Kao could say was, 'They've got Rahman.'

---

[15] Abdul Mannan, 'The Big Bird and Narratives of a General', *Daily Sun*, 26 March 2018.

Chapter 8

Pervious Borders

STEADY GUNFIRE; ONE SHOT EVERY TEN SECONDS.

The West Pakistani Army was merciless. There were only wails and cries, destruction and death.

'Kill three million of them and the rest will eat out of our hands,'[16] Yahya Khan had declared grandly. Yahya's sole purpose was the suppression of East Pakistan. What had started as a political strategy to overthrow the elected government had now become a full-fledged military occupation.

Once they had Sheikh Mujibur Rahman in their custody, the Pakistani military descended on residential localities; houses were looted and set on fire. People were gunned down as they ran out of their homes. Women raped, shot and hung from the heels. Children slaughtered. The carnage was indiscriminate.

---

[16] Philip Hensher, 'The War Bangladesh Can Never Forget', *The Independent*, 19 February 2013.

The reports that would come in later, from Intelligence agents as well as the international media, would describe horrific acts of violence across East Pakistan—torture, people being burned alive or shot, some of them killed in their sleep. From his office in Dhaka, Tikka Khan orchestrated a terrible symphony of mass murder.

Zulfikar Ali Bhutto was in Dhaka too on the night of 25 March. As the city burned, he stood in his hotel room in the Sheraton, watching with pleasure the atrocities committed by the Pakistani Army.

This was Operation Searchlight, Pakistan's armed suppression of East Bengal. They wanted to stop the resistance once and for all. The total annihilation of the Bengalis in East Pakistan was what they were aiming for. Soon, it became evident that the Bengalis were completely at the mercy of the non-Bengalis. Bengali areas in Old Dhaka were burned down. Hindus were undeniably the preferred targets of the Pakistani Army.

The death toll increased every day. At first, the casualties numbered in the hundreds, then in the thousands, and finally, lakhs. The East Pakistani population knew now that they had to fight back. They did not have an option. It was genocide, and they simply could not remain silent as their country and their people burned.

The soldiers from the East Bengal Regiment of the Pakistani Army defected and took it upon themselves to defend their Bengali brethren. Gun battles on the streets became the order of the day. What Pakistan had thought would be a quick, surgical suppression of the demand for independence had turned into a civil war.

As the days passed, the Bengali population gave it a name. Muktijuddho. The war for freedom.

◻

As East Pakistan faced its darkest night, Indira Gandhi expressed her sympathy and anguish to its people. During Operation Searchlight, India became the nearest refuge for the Bengalis who were forced to flee their country. People came in small and large numbers, seeking shelter.

The first parliamentary resolution regarding East Pakistan was passed in the Indian Parliament on 31 March 1971. It said, 'The people of East Bengal are being sought to be suppressed by the naked use of force by bayonets, machine guns, tanks, artillery and aircraft.' The House also 'called upon all peoples and governments of the world to take urgent and constructive steps to prevail upon the Government of Pakistan to put an end immediately to the systematic decimation of people which amounts to genocide.' The House had a 'profound conviction that the historic upsurge of the seventy-five million people of East Bengal will triumph. The House wishes to assure them that their struggle and sacrifices will receive the wholehearted sympathy and support of the people of India.'[17]

The resolution carefully avoided committing India to an active role in bringing about a settlement in East Pakistan, but the border gates of India were opened up for the persecuted East Bengalis.

Meanwhile, the number of killings increased by the day, and on 4 April 1971, the East Pakistan forces came together to form the Bangladesh armed forces. They were led by Colonel M.A.G. Osmani, later known as Bongobir, or the hero of Bengal.

Osmani had initiated the creation and organisation of the rebel military committee in December 1970. He had had the foresight to formulate a comprehensive plan to seize power from West Pakistan if political negotiations failed. However, his plans didn't materialise as Tikka Khan took East Pakistan by surprise with the attacks that started on 25 March. Col. Osmani then stepped up and offered to become the commander-in-chief for the defecting East Pakistani army.

Kao realised that this was India's opportunity to enter the scene. They already had a massive amount of manpower at their disposal, in the form of the millions

---

[17] Robert Jackson, *South Asian Crisis: India–Pakistan–Bangla Desh* (Palgrave Macmillan, UK, 1975), p. 171.

of refugees pouring into the country. Most of them had fought against the Pakistan government in one way or another before finding themselves outgunned, outnumbered and forced to flee. Some of them were soldiers of the East Bengal Regiment of the Pakistani Army. These men were not only well-trained but also had knowledge about the Pakistani military's modus operandi.

A plan started to take shape at the R&AW headquarters.

'We need to be intelligent here,' Kao told Nair. 'We're not preparing for a full-scale military assault. But we do need to hit them where it hurts.'

'Guerrilla tactics?' Nair asked.

'Exactly,' Kao said with a smile. 'Our actions need to be based on Intelligence.'

'The refugees themselves are a valuable resource on that front,' Nair replied.

'Which is why I want you to go back down there and set up a system where each willing refugee is debriefed in detail,' Kao said. 'Get everything they know, no matter how small the detail, so that we can base our actions on the information we obtain. The prime minister will sanction our move soon. But we need to start preparing in advance.'

A decision was taken to create a non-conventional fighting force by training a large set of volunteers within a short time. These guerrilla fighters would be sent back into East Pakistan with specific instructions to adopt hit-and-run tactics to weaken enemy morale. They would be accompanied by another group that would not take part in frontal attacks. These men would be trained to gather information on the enemy.

Kao and Nair found that there was no shortage of people willing to join the fight for East Pakistan. The number of volunteers who wanted to be recruited into the guerrilla force continued to increase, and by the end of April, it had risen to 250,000.

◻

In any country or situation, an exodus of refugees is similar in its structure. For the most part, the refugees are scared and clueless. Only a few of them are able to take stock of the crisis, rise to the occasion and assume leadership. They round up their people, identify escape routes and decide on the best times to make their move. Often, these leaders stay back in dangerous places and situations to help the next lot of refugees escape.

During Operation Searchlight, this job fell to the members and supporters of the Awami League. Rahman was under arrest and India had rescued his close aides, but the other members of the party were still on the ground. They understood that the party leaders had to be protected so that a proper government could be formed after victory was achieved.

Tajuddin Ahmed, Mujibur Rahman's trusted aide and long-time member of the Awami League, had crossed into India from East Pakistan on 30 March, along with his companion Syed Nazrul Islam, and sought political asylum. He and Islam were taken first to Calcutta and then to Delhi, where Gandhi herself met them. Tajuddin appealed to the Indian government to carve out 'a liberated area' near the India–East Pakistan border. Tajuddin's request was approved by Gandhi. She wanted India to be instrumental in charting the course of events for the liberation of East Pakistan. She also wanted to ensure that the resources the Indian government had provided to this end were being used judiciously.

On 10 April, the Provisional Government of Bangladesh issued a proclamation on the basis of the previous declaration of independence by Rahman, and a government-in-exile, called the People's Republic of Bangladesh, was formed. Sheikh Mujibur Rahman was named president of the republic, Syed Nazrul Islam was vice president, and Tajuddin Ahmed officiated as prime minister. Tajuddin would be in charge in Rahman's absence. The new Bangladeshi government was formed in a town called Mujibnagar; its capital in exile was Calcutta. After the formation of the exile government, the Awami League started spreading the news amongst the Bangladeshi refugees to boost their morale. Covert meetings were held in the dead of night, and messages were passed across borders. The refugees were told that help was on the way, but they needed to become the eyes and ears of the government-in-exile in Calcutta.

On 29 April 1971, the Government of India requested the Indian Army to take over the responsibility of assisting the Bangladeshi forces in their war for liberation. In the guise of Col. Menon, Nair travelled east to survey the training of the guerrilla fighters. Nearly twenty-five secret 'youth' camps, each with a training capacity of around 1,000 men, had been set up near the East Pakistan borders. The men were trained in weapon-handling, field-craft, raids and ambushes, commando operations and the use of small radio sets. They also underwent basic medical training.

A system was worked out wherein Intelligence about the current situation in Bangladesh, including the positions, movements and resources of the Pakistan military, would be passed on to India through incoming refugees. Awami League members were cautioned against putting all their eggs in one basket, and they agreed to identify and assign five to six people in each batch of refugees to the job. The tactic worked like magic, mainly because the people of East Pakistan had already come to see India as their ally and believed it was their patriotic duty to help the Indian government in any way possible. After all, India was helping them in their war for independence. When the situation in East Pakistan had started deteriorating, R&AW agents previously inserted in the region had also worked towards reinforcing the belief that India was Bangladesh's friend in this time of crisis. India had wanted to win the hearts and minds of East Bengal's people before playing tactical games, and it had succeeded. Kao's strategy was being quietly put to use without any fanfare.

It was classic Kao. Results, not words.

□

Nair reached the tent which served as the command post for the training camp. A stack of reports was on a table before him. The junior officer who had received him stood to attention just beyond the table.

'Where are we?' Nair asked.

'They're raw, but they're motivated, sir. We're training them the best we can. May I ask … what news from Delhi, sir?'

Nair removed his glasses, laid them on the table and pinched the bridge of his nose.

'They're politicians,' he said. 'They'll take their own sweet time.'

In Delhi, Prime Minister Indira Gandhi was sitting silently in her office, lost in thought. Gandhi knew that the world was looking towards India to take a stand. She was weighing all her options before sending the Indian Army into Bangladesh.

As the days passed, the Intelligence started coming in. Sitting in his tent, Nair patiently read all the reports and began mapping out critical locations on a map of Bangladesh. Details about deployment were jotted down in the margins. Routes along the porous border were selected based on their proximity to the target locations. Teams were created on paper. Details of training modules for the rebel fighters were finalised.

'Teach them to identify targets,' Nair said. 'They need to know what they're looking for. And they have to strike fast. Above all, teach them the importance of a strategic retreat. They need to know that there's no shame in running away so that they can live to fight another day. All the patriotism in the world isn't going to do them any good if they're dead.'

Officers with the BSF, which had been operating as a front for R&AW since Muktijuddho started, combed the refugee camps and began singling out potential recruits: men and women who were reasonably fit, between the ages of eighteen and thirty-five.

'How are we proposing to send them back in?' Nair asked the commanding officer at the BSF facility.

'The same way they came, sir. The borders are very porous right now. The Pakistani military has its hands full and border security isn't exactly a priority right now.'

'Send them in through the waterways,' Nair said. 'The Pakistani Army won't know how to navigate these waters. A large number of men in the rebel recruits are farmers. They've lived and worked around the labyrinth of East Pakistan's rivers. Let them use their knowledge of the terrain to their advantage.' He continued, 'How are the men here handling the weapons?'

'They're learning. It helps that they're very motivated. Half of them still have families stuck in East Pakistan and are anxious to get back, if only to check whether they're still alive.'

The rebels were prepped and sent into Bangladesh via the water channels. They used the intimate knowledge they had of Bangladesh's environment to their advantage.

◻

Meanwhile, Gandhi had visited Assam, Tripura and West Bengal to get a sense of the realities of Operation Searchlight, and she soon realised it was nothing short of genocide. She was so overwhelmed by the reports of the massacre across the border that she could hardly speak. She held a Cabinet meeting in her office. Apart from external affairs minister Sardar Swaran Singh, agriculture minister Fakhruddin Ali Ahmad, defence minister Babu Jagjivan Ram and finance minister Yashwant Rao Chavan, India's chief of army staff, Sam Manekshaw was present. When Gandhi suggested that the Indian Army enter Pakistan, Sam Manekshaw was adamant that this was not the right move to make at the time. The main reason he cited for postponing action was that an unprovoked military step from India's side would make India look like the aggressor.

Also, Manekshaw felt the Army was not prepared to go to war. For one, the Himalayan passes were opening up, and there could be an attack from China. Also, an armoured division and two of his infantry divisions were away. He would need tremendous resources in terms of road and railway transport to move these divisions to the operational areas. Another deterrent he cited was the impending monsoons. 'The monsoons are monstrous in East Pakistan and Bengal. The whole countryside will get flooded. The snows are melting, and the rivers will become like oceans. … All the movement would be confined to roads. The Air Force, because of climatic conditions, would not be able to support me.'[18]

Manekshaw looked around the room; everyone in it, including the prime minister, was hanging on his every word.

---

[18] Directorate General of Infantry, *Field Marshall KM Kariappa Memorial Lectures, 1995–2000* (Lancer Publishers, New Delhi, 2001), p. 29.

'Now, Prime Minister, give me your orders,' he said.

Indira Gandhi realised that an immediate war was out of the question. Manekshaw needed time to prepare for war, and Gandhi, Haksar and Kao would have to find a way to give him that time.

The men of the rebel camp, trained in guerrilla tactics, were the answer. But they needed resources.

◻

'Didn't you once mention an Israeli gentleman you met in London?' Kao asked Haksar.

The two men were meeting in the latter's office. The guerrilla force was taking shape slowly and steadily, but a major issue remained. Kao was hoping to sort it out that day.

'Shlomo Zabludowicz,' Haksar said promptly.

Zabludowicz was a Polish Jew and a survivor of the concentration camp at Auschwitz, one of the most infamous death camps that the Holocaust had seen. Haksar and Zabludowicz had become friends when Haksar was posted as deputy high commissioner in London in 1965.

Kao's idea was based on a recent statement released by Israel, which publicly pledged support to the people of East Pakistan and lashed out against the atrocities being committed by the Pakistani Army in the region—and for good reason. Having gone through unspeakable horrors themselves, the people of Israel found themselves relating deeply to the plight of the people of East Pakistan.

'We need ammunition for the rebel recruits,' Kao told Haksar. 'From a source that can't be traced back to us directly.'

Haksar leaned back in his seat. He saw Kao's point. Israel would be more than willing to help East Pakistan, and the resilient nation would also figure out a way to smuggle the arsenal across to the guerrilla force.

'Anything in particular that you need?' Haksar asked.

'Heavy weaponry. Mortars. That's the priority if we want our guerrilla force to gain an upper hand in the fight.'

'I'll see what I can do,' Haksar said.

Haksar reached out to Zabludowicz, who promised to help. He, in turn, passed the request on to Israeli prime minister Golda Meir, who was eager to help her Indian counterpart, Indira Gandhi.

The weapons made their way to India from Israel in absolute secrecy. This was also the beginning of a long friendship between the two countries.

◻

It was past midnight. There was a deathly silence in the air; even the crickets had stopped chirping. The smell of smoke was everywhere, as was the smell of burning flesh.

Just hours ago, a squad of Pakistani soldiers had stormed into a small village in East Pakistan and turned it into a morgue. Every single human being was hunted down and killed. Houses were set on fire. A pile was made of all the Bangla literature that they had found and used for a campfire.

Silently, the guerrilla leader peeked over the compound wall of the building where his team had taken cover, and took stock of the situation. Seven soldiers were sitting around the fire, eating from their rations. Three others were on guard duty, patrolling the perimeter of the temporary camp. Then the guerrilla leader slipped back into the shadows.

'I count ten, but there might be others. Also, an army truck.'

The others nodded and checked their assault rifles. The leader turned around and raised his hand, holding three fingers up. One finger went down, then another, and then he knifed his hand forward.

Silently, the team of fifteen men ran forward in the darkness till they reached the edge of the light from the burning buildings. Two of the three Pakistani soldiers on patrol duty saw them first.

'JOY BANGLA!' the leader screamed.

Fifteen AK-47 assault rifles boomed in near-perfect unison. The Pakistani soldiers were cut down before they could even realise what was happening. The guerrilla team walked among the dead bodies, some of them spitting on the corpses, checking for survivors. A couple of them went over to the truck. Working quickly, they removed the arms and ammunition they found inside and set the truck on fire.

A third went over to a half-burned building that the Pakistani soldiers had raided hours earlier. Using a piece of chalk, the guerrilla warrior wrote two words in large Bengali letters on the wall:

MUKTI BAHINI.

The force had a name. They were the liberation army.

Chapter 9

A Game of Foxes

Bangla Desh, Bangla Desh,
Where so many people are dying fast,
And it sure looks like a mess,
I've never seen such distress,
Now won't you lend your hand, try to understand,
Relieve the people of Bangladesh.[19]

IT WAS THE EVENING OF 1 AUGUST 1971. A SUMMER breeze blew over a sombre crowd of 40,000 gathered at Madison Square Garden in New York City for the benefit concert organised by musicians George Harrison and Ravi Shankar. The song, *Bangla Desh*, that George Harrison was singing had connected millions of people by evoking one sentiment: humanity. Against every expectation, over 40,000 people had turned up for the concert, and $250,000 was raised in a single day. The money was intended as aid for the refugee crisis.

---

[19] Lyrics of the song *Bangla Desh* by George Harrison.

Back in April, after Indira Gandhi had taken the decision to postpone the war, a plan had been devised to engage Pakistan in guerrilla, information and PR warfare until all preparations for war had been completed. Kao had realised that the training camps and the armed resistance headed by the Mukti Bahini were not going to be enough. They would have to set their 'information management' plan in motion. By this time, Pakistan had been getting increasingly loud in its accusations against India, declaring that their neighbour was exploiting the conflict in East Pakistan for their own ends. The US was well aware of the turmoil and bloodshed in East Pakistan, but President Nixon and his security adviser Henry Kissinger had chosen to look away.

From the time Operation Searchlight had been unleashed on the East Pakistanis, Archer Blood, the American consul general in East Pakistan, had sent angry telegrams to several American consulate offices and embassies around the world, expressing extreme horror at the systematic massacre of Bengali civilians by Pakistani troops. He also sent telegrams to the Department of State, condemning the failure of the US to denounce the widespread atrocities and the suppression of democracy in East Pakistan. However, Nixon and Kissinger rejected these missives, which came to be known as the Blood Telegrams. With the White House averting its eyes, the Pakistani Army killed around 300,000 Bengalis, most of them Hindus, and forced 10 million to flee to India.

At the time, Nixon and Kissinger were trying to establish diplomatic relations with China. Pakistan and, in particular, Yahya Khan, had become Nixon's secret liaison with China. Thus, the US not only refused to condemn Yahya Khan and Operation Searchlight, but also declined to withhold the supply of American arms and ammunition that kept Pakistan's military machine throbbing.

Nixon and Kissinger had a soft spot for Yahya Khan. 'A man's man,' they called him. 'He wasn't some woman running a country.'[20] This was an obvious jibe directed at Indira Gandhi. It was evident that Nixon wanted Pakistan to be protected at all costs, and to prevent India from emerging as the dominant power in South Asia.

At the R&AW office, Kao and his team sat together to plan their next course of action. Kao had been toying with ways to counter the constant onslaught of propaganda from Pakistan.

'Remember what we talked about when this whole thing started?' Kao asked.

'Yes. It's time to put our plan of psychological warfare into action,' Nair said.

---

[20] Gary J. Bass, *The Blood Telegram: India's Secret War in East Pakistan* (Alfred A. Knopf, New York, 2013), p. 12.

Since the beginning of the genocide in East Pakistan, R&AW had successfully leaked information to the Indian press about the countless atrocities suffered by the people in East Pakistan. Almost every day, some newspaper or other carried a feature on Tikka Khan's use of brute force to suppress the Muktijuddho.

It was, Kao decided, time to step it up.

The first thing that Indira Gandhi did in this direction, on Haksar and Kao's advice, was to start writing letters to world leaders, apprising them of the situation on the border. Simultaneously, Kao set about taking the press coverage of the situation to the international level. Feelers were sent out, indicating that any member of the press in a Western country who sought to cover the on-ground situation in East Pakistan would be extended every courtesy and cooperation by the Government of India. Indian diplomats and bureaucrats reached out to their counterparts in the West, calling in favours or seeking new ones, making it known that any journalist who wished to speak to the East Bengali refugees in India was more than welcome to do so.

Eventually, foreign reporters who wanted a closer look at East Pakistan were smuggled into conflict zones under the protection of the Mukti Bahini, so that they could cover the actual story and not the version that the Pakistan government was presenting to the world.

The article that truly changed world opinion towards East Pakistan was 'Genocide', by Anthony Mascarenhas, which was published by UK's *Sunday Times*. It was an exposé on the situation in East Pakistan, and the extent of the brutality of the Pakistan military. The article was published on 13 June 1971.

Thousands of families of unfortunate Muslims, many of them refugees from Bihar who chose Pakistan at the time of the partition riots in 1947, were mercilessly wiped out. Women were raped, or had their breasts torn out with specially fashioned knives. Children did not escape the horror: the lucky ones were killed with their parents; but many thousands of others must go through what life remains for them with eyes gouged out and limbs roughly amputated. More than 20,000 bodies of non-Bengalis have been found in the main towns, such as Chittagong, Khulna and Jessore. The real toll, I was told everywhere in East Bengal, may have been as high as 100,000; for thousands of non-Bengalis have vanished without a trace. … No meaningful or viable political solution is possible in East Bengal while the pogrom continues. The crucial question is: Will the killing stop?[21]

---

[21] Anthony Mascarenhas, 'Genocide', *The Daily Star*, 16 December 2017.

The article was widely read and talked about—the pre-internet equivalent of 'going viral'—and prompted the International Rescue Committee to send an emergency mission to India to conduct its own study of the matter. Its report, titled 'Escape from Terror', pointed out, 'Preoccupied with the basic needs of refugees, i.e. food, shelter and first-aid, the (Indian) governmental assistance program, though substantial, cannot cope with the multi-faceted organisational and financial needs described in the foregoing pages.'[22]

The seeds had been sown in the right places. Across the world, the media was informing people about the apathy and brutality of the Pakistan government, as well as making them realise that India could no longer bear, alone, the brunt of the massacre and the mass exodus from East Bengal. The benefit concert for Bangladesh by Ravi Shankar and George Harrison was also a step in this direction—popular culture was an effective tool to spread information.

The sustained media campaign that R&AW had started also changed the role India was playing in the world's eyes. From an aggressor, India was being seen

---

[22] International Rescue Committee, *Escape from Terror, A Report of the International Rescue Committee Emergency Mission to India for Pakistan Refugees*, submitted on 28 July 1971 by its chairman Angier B. Duke to F.L. Kellogg, Special Assistant to the Secretary of State for Refugee Affairs, Government of USA (New York, NY, International Rescue Committee, 1971).

as a country that was simply trying to help out on humanitarian grounds.

India's foreign affairs minister, Sardar Swaran Singh, had started his advocacy campaign too, undertaking a tour to several cities in North America, from the month of July 1971. Cabinet minister K.C. Pant visited several countries in Asia and Central America. Mohammad Yunus of the Indian Foreign Service, also a close friend of Indira Gandhi, toured the Islamic countries to argue and advocate for India.

The agenda had been simple and clear: to emphasise the need to pressure the Pakistan government into offering a political solution in East Pakistan that was acceptable to the Awami League, if peace and stability were to be preserved in South Asia.

Tajuddin Ahmed, too, appealed to the world for aid, for recognition of the Bangladeshi cause, and for Sheikh Mujibur Rahman's safety.

When Rahman had been arrested on the night of 25 March 1971, he had been driven to the residence of Tikka Khan in Dhaka. There, he had been confined in a room for six days. During this period, his whereabouts were unknown to the world, for the Pakistani Army had made sure that his location was kept under tight wraps. In April, Rahman had been flown to Rawalpindi, where he was moved to Mianwali Prison and put in a condemned cell. West Pakistan's military government had begun proceedings against him on twelve charges, six of which carried the death penalty. The gravest of these charges was 'waging war against Pakistan'.

The effects of R&AW's media campaign about East Pakistan and Rahman's treatment at the hands of his captors had started to become apparent by June.

A crowd of around twenty-five thousand protestors gathered at Trafalgar Square in London, urging the Pakistan government to stop the genocide and free Bangladesh. This was an important protest as it was covered extensively by the British media, and it indicated that other nations too were accepting Bangladesh as a new nation. This protest was followed by demonstrations in various parts of the world against the Pakistan government.

Pakistan didn't back down from trying to control the narrative either. They continued their own media onslaught against India. They were still confident of their two powerful allies—China and the US.

However, the international media had stopped being kind by then. The US received mail from Berlin, with no return addresses, asking for the recognition of the 'People's Republic of Bangladesh'. The American government was also under pressure from their own citizens. Massive rallies were held in New York. Despite this, though, Nixon pledged to support Pakistan and Yahya Khan. Nixon proclaimed, 'It is most unfortunate that this humanitarian question should be cynically turned into political propaganda by India, and that the Indian government should use the problem of displaced persons as an instrument of pressure on Pakistan to impose a political government of Indian choice in East Pakistan. No government could yield to such blackmail.'[23]

America's alliance with Pakistan had its roots in events that occurred long before Indira Gandhi came to power. During the Cold War, India had chosen to follow a policy of non-alignment, a decision that the US viewed as being on par with siding with the USSR.

During the 1962 war against China, although Kennedy did not give Nehru everything he asked for, he did send C-130s, automatic weapons and ammunition. This assistance continued even after India was defeated by China. But when Pakistan attacked India in 1965, in an explosion of the Kashmir dispute, the US was in the awkward position of having to provide arms to both sides.

China had automatically become an ally of Pakistan after the 1962 conflict with India. Subsequently, it had stepped up the supply of arms and ammunition to Pakistan. Unfortunately for India, the US decided

---

[23] Louis J. Smith, ed., 'Foreign Relations of the United States, 1969–1976', *South Asia Crisis, 1971 Volume XI* (United States Government Printing Office, Washington, 2005), p. 192.

to use Pakistan as a mediator to reach a diplomatic resolution with China. Thus, in the event of a war between India and Pakistan, the US would neither be able to support India nor remain a peacemaker.

China, too, in the light of their conflict with the Soviet Union after the Cultural Revolution, found it most convenient to respond positively to overtures from the US. Since China and the US explicitly sided with Pakistan on the Bangladesh issue, India was now up against a powerful US–China–Pak axis.

◻

Yahya Khan, in the cocoon of protection provided by the US and China, kept the carnage going in Bangladesh. In fact, unsatisfied with Gen. Tikka Khan's performance, Yahya Khan even had him replaced in April 1971. The officer who succeeded him was a junior-ranking officer—Gen. A.A.K. Niazi.

Gen. Niazi and his team uncovered information about the clandestine training camps of the guerrilla force that was fighting to liberate Bangladesh. They had pinpointed twenty-nine camps within India where guerrillas were being trained. Yahya was told they even had a name—Mukti Bahini.

Yahya Khan decided to keep the aggression going in Bangladesh to suppress any and all resistance. However, the Mukti Bahini's guerrilla tactics continued to plague the Pakistani military. The guerrillas were a valiant bunch, deeply motivated by the nationalist cause. They were averaging eighteen Pakistanis a day, and blowing up railway lines and bridges and bravely facing down the Pakistani Army.

Yahya Khan was at his wits' end. There was no respite in sight. The Bangladeshis were refusing to back down, and they also had India's support. Yahya Khan was losing men and resources, and Pakistan's image was tarnished by the world media. Systematically, Pakistan's lies about Bangladesh were exposed in the world media. They could no longer evade being called the 'aggressor'. India had played her game well.

But, on the other hand, every day, the Mukti Bahini was losing almost as much ground as it was capturing. The problem wasn't that they weren't motivated or committed enough. The difficulty, to put it simply, was that they were not soldiers.

'You can't make a soldier in a month, after all,' Nair said, when he met Kao to discuss the matter in the latter's office. 'There's a reason why recruits into the armed forces undergo such a lengthy and rigorous training programme. It takes time to drum into them the principles that come with a uniform.'

Kao nodded. He understood all too well the difference between a trained soldier and a rebel outlaw.

'But we do have some trained ones, don't we?' Kao was thinking aloud.

'Not many, in comparison with the entire force.'

'Separate them,' Kao said. 'Take them to a different location. As soon as possible.'

'Okay, but it won't be done in a day. Some of them are out there on missions as we speak and won't be back for days.'

'Recall them. Use whatever means necessary.'

As Nair had warned, it took some time, but within a month, all the former soldiers of the East Pakistani Army who had defected after Bangladesh declared itself an independent country were sequestered in a separate training camp run by the Indian Army. For the next two months, they were put through a gruelling training session, physical and psychological, where it was impressed upon them that they were the tip of the spear in the war to liberate Bangladesh. It was a huge responsibility, they were told, but their country needed them to step up and take on the challenge.

When they returned to the secret base camp set up near the border after their training, they were different men. They were then divided into various specialised forces and teams.

The Niyomito Bahini or regular force would conduct frontal attacks on the enemy. The Gano Bahini would be the support system—running guerrilla camps inside enemy territory, ferrying supplies and tending to the wounded. These forces would never lose sight of the most crucial objective of all: Intelligence gathering. There was also an irregular force, comprising the suicide squad and the scorpion squad. The suicide squad was tasked with killing prominent workers who were accomplices of the Pakistan government— members of the Muslim League, the Razakars and the government officials themselves. They were trained to kill themselves when in danger of being captured by the enemy. The bichhu or scorpion squad consisted of women who were trained to carry out espionage assignments.

The special squad that was expertly handled by Kao and the R&AW themselves was a new force—the Mujib Bahini. Kao understood that some men were simply more motivated than others, like those closest to Sheikh Mujibur Rahman. These were members of the Awami League who had spent years fighting for their rights alongside Bangabandhu, and had become his closest associates, even friends. The Mujib Bahini was thoroughly committed to Mujibur Rahman and believed passionately in his ideology. The elite force was headed by Sheikh Fazlul Haque Mani, a student leader of the Awami League and Rahman's nephew.

One of the primary purposes of the Mujib Bahini was to keep a check on the Maoists of East Bengal from penetrating the Mukti Bahini and other Bahinis. The East Bengali Maoists were believed to have links to the

Chinese Communist Party. If left unchecked, through these elements, China, who was Pakistan's ally, could take control of the Mukti Bahini, jeopardising the movement for independence.

If the Niyomito Bahini was the tip of the spear, the Mujib Bahini was the ideological guardian of the Muktijuddho.

□

The Mujib Bahini was created under the supervision of the chief of the SFF, Maj. Gen. Uban, who reported directly to Kao and R&AW. Uban was a legendary figure, a Military Cross awardee who had commanded a Long Range Desert Group Squadron in North Africa during World War II. He was the chosen foreman for the mission.

'The whole movement hinges on the beliefs of their leader, Mujibur Rahman,' Kao told Nair. 'If those beliefs are punctured, the whole thing will come crashing down around us. I'm not saying the ultra-leftists are trying to take over. I'm just saying that the possibility has to be acknowledged.'

'I understand,' Nair said. 'But will the others in the force?'

Kao knew what Nair meant.

Members of the Mujib Bahini had been selected not just based on their closeness to Rahman, but also after a thorough interview in which their political leanings were gauged. This had created an apparent lack of trust within the force, provoking some gossip about the Mujib Bahini and their proximity to R&AW. The fact that the Mujib Bahini was provided better training and equipment than the other squads of the Mukti Bahini also fuelled the gossip mill. The former answered directly to R&AW, unlike the other teams which reported to the Bangladeshi government-in-exile or to Col. Osmani. Consequently, a discord had developed between the elite squad and the rest of the force that provided them with logistical support.

'How are we going to deal with the discontent?' Nair asked.

'By ending this struggle as fast as possible,' Kao said. 'When they win, this will be referred to as but a minor detail in the larger scheme of things. Once they win their independence, this won't matter.'

'*If* they win,' Nair said.

'No,' Kao said, looking squarely at Nair. '*If* is no longer an option.'

India was now heavily involved and leading the war for the liberation of Bangladesh.

Chapter 10

Wreckage by Design

THE COMMANDO CROUCHED BEHIND THE BUSHES, gun raised, sweat glazing his forehead. Behind him, his fourteen-member team was spread out. Not too far, not too close. Cover was scarce in this terrain. They had to work with what they had, just as they had done for the last twenty days.

In front of the commando was a Pakistani Army soldier relieving himself. Behind him, his team was poised to act, but only if necessary; the leader had been given strict instructions to stick to their mission and refrain from engaging in violent attacks.

For three months, the commando and his team had planned for the top-secret assignment. Now, they were close to accomplishing their mission, too close to let it be jeopardised.

The Pakistan Army soldier took his time, zipping up his fly and adjusting his belt lazily, as the commando leader exchanged looks with his team members. They were all thinking the same thing. There were residential areas nearby. A gunshot or even a shout, if it was loud enough, was bound to attract attention.

'We can't fail now, Ya Allah,' the commando thought to himself. 'Not now. Not after everything we've gone through.'

The commando's mission, which was in its final stages that night in August 1971, had had its genesis in March, aboard a Pakistani naval submarine docked in Toulon in France. The new submarine, PNS *Mangro*, had just been built for Pakistan in France, and among the crew were thirteen ethnic Bengalis. On 26 March 1971, the Bengali crew listened to the radio, shocked, as Tikka Khan started his slaughter in East Pakistan. There was a declaration of independence from Sheikh Mujibur Rahman and a message to East Pakistanis to keep fighting.

Their hearts bled, but they were so far away from their country that there was little they could do. They knew they were outnumbered, and hence hijacking the submarine was not really an option. So, nine members of the Bengali crew on board the submarine came up with a plan to defect and make their way from Europe into India. They packed their valuables and had them shipped to East Pakistan so that no one would suspect anything. They then found their window of opportunity and escaped. Soon, the news spread that the Bengali naval crew had abandoned the Pakistani ship.

The French secret service was assigned to the task of finding them and bringing them back. The defectors had a thrilling and at times harrowing experience as they made their way across France and four other European nations, before they finally managed to reach India.

In Delhi, they were questioned at length by R&AW. Kao had instructed his men to make sure that the crew was passionate about the Bangladesh cause before giving them sanctuary. Once R&AW had thoroughly interrogated them, they were granted political asylum. The crew also shared sensitive information about the Pakistani Navy with R&AW.

It was decided then that the men would form a naval commando unit and take part in a meticulously planned operation that would cripple West Pakistan's naval command over East Pakistan. The former crew members of PNS *Mangro* were thus recruited to the Mukti Bahini under Col. Osmani.

□

At the time, Kao and Indira Gandhi were walking a perilous tightrope. Covertly, they were doing everything they could to extend support to the Muktijuddho. But officially, their hands were tied. Any overt gesture of support for East Pakistan would be seen as an act of aggression in the eyes of the world, and Pakistan would never stop playing the victim if that happened. Moreover, the US and China were waiting for a reason to lash out at India.

Kao and Gandhi had discussed this for hours before coming to a single conclusion: Pakistan had to be forced into making the first move. And they had to make that happen as fast as they could. Kao decided to step up the pressure through the attacks by the Mukti Bahini.

It was during this time that the names 'Mukti Bahini' and 'R&AW' began to be used interchangeably by the Indian armed forces.

The guerrilla force was supplied with mortars to up the scale of the destruction. Smooth bore guns for firing shells or bombs were included in the next supply of artillery to the Gano Bahini. While the Niyomito Bahini took care of the frontal attacks, the Gano Bahini operated the mortars and did the auxiliary damage.

Simultaneously, specialised training was imparted to the naval commando unit of the Mukti Bahini. Naval commandos who had defected to join the Muktijuddho, about 160 of them, were pulled off their current missions. They were given a new task—sinking ships.

West Pakistan had two routes to reach East Pakistan: airways and the Indian Ocean. India had successfully prohibited their air travel through Indian airspace, and now the plan was to cripple their access to the water as well. This mission was named Operation Jackpot.

Commodore Abdul Wahed Chowdhary, one of the defecting Bengali submariners, led the team as the chief of Operation Jackpot. He was able to use the expertise he had gained as a submariner on PNS *Ghazi* in 1964. After the 1971 war, he would serve in important positions of the Bangladesh Navy, as the director of naval intelligence and as a member of the National Committee.

Additionally, the best swimmers from the Mukti Bahini camps were handpicked by the Indian Navy. They underwent specialised training for up to eighteen hours a day—a rigorous module that included swimming, night swimming, underwater swimming, underwater demolition, night demolition, object demolition training, the use of limpet mines, survival training, and hand-to-hand combat, among other things. Limpet mines, especially, required advanced training. These magnetic naval mines that are used to damage ships below the waterline are hard to handle, and swimmers have to carry them on their chest.

Slowly, Kao built a navy for the Mukti Bahini. By the time the monsoon had arrived in India and East Pakistan, the commandos were ready.

The monsoon season, extending from June to September, favoured guerrilla tactics. Two-thirds of East Pakistan was waterlogged during these months, limiting mobility on roads, railways and river craft. The India–East Pakistan border was around 2,000-kilometres long and devoid of natural obstacles. Several roads and railway lines were close to the border and vulnerable to attack. The interior of East Pakistan could be reached easily by guerrillas from the border areas via river ways and delta channels.

The Mukti Bahini took full advantage of the weather. The monsoon restricted the Pakistani Army's mobility, but the guerrillas continued to mount small, deep raids from their sanctuaries in India as well as from remote border enclaves. The number of raids increased during the rains, as did the wreckage and terror they caused. No less than 1,371 ambushes were organised in the monsoon of 1971. A steady attack on public property continued. The onslaught damaged 123 road and rail bridges, derailed 12 trains, and destroyed 31 sections of railway tracks as well as 149 sections of telegraph and telephone lines and poles. Detachments of the Pakistani Army were attacked by the Mukti Bahini, causing more than 1,000 casualties, which were duly reported by the foreign press. The Pakistani Army was then forced to use vicious counter-insurgency tactics, which increased the hostility of the disaffected East Pakistani population.

It was during this monsoon that the date for Operation Jackpot was set.

The operation, which would go down in the annals of history as one of the most successful naval missions ever to be conducted, was planned for the last week of July. Only a handful of people were to be involved in the planning phase. Information on river tides, weather, and East Pakistan's naval infrastructure and deployment was collected through the Mukti Bahini. Selected commandos were sent to forward bases in Tripura and West Bengal, where a final briefing was given to them. One group would go to Chittagong, another to Chandpur and Narayanganj, and the third to Mongla. The mission of the operation was to launch simultaneous attacks in four ports: Chittagong, Mongla, Chandpur and Narayanganj.

Taking advantage of the abundance of rivers in East Pakistan, the three groups left in the dead of night in boats. Each commando was equipped with a pair of fins, a knife, a limpet mine and swimming trunks. Some had compasses, and one in three commandos carried sten guns and hand grenades. Their food supplies were limited. The group leaders also carried transistor radios.

The commandos set off on their respective expeditions on 27 July 1971. They had an arduous journey ahead, as they would have to traverse the

Sunderban delta to reach their destination ports. They were under strict orders not to engage enemy targets en route unless it was absolutely necessary.

They almost always travelled at night, lying low during the day at safe houses set up over months. They used the daylight hours to stock up on their food and water rations with the help of undercover R&AW agents and Mukti Bahini members.

The journey lasted more than two weeks. They silently made their way into enemy territory, warding off tigers and crocodiles, slipping past the Pakistani Army's eyes, and keeping their morale up, even as their supplies dwindled and physical ailments took over.

During this time of extreme physical and emotional hardship, the one thing that kept them motivated was listening to pre-recorded speeches of their beloved Bangabandhu on the Swadhin Betar Bangla radio channel.

The Swadhin Betar Bangla first came to prominence when Sheikh Mujibur Rahman broadcast a message to the people of East Pakistan, inspiring them to keep up the freedom struggle even after his arrest on 25 March 1971. Two days later, on 27 March, Maj. Ziaur Rahman had proclaimed an independent Bangladesh from this very radio station. It continued broadcasting in bold defiance of the military regime till the Pakistani

Air Force (PAF) bombed the station in Chittagong, destroying it.

Nevertheless, a group of radio artists managed to cross the border and revive the channel in India. They resumed transmissions from the headquarters of the provisional government set up in Calcutta on 25 May 1971. Later, after receiving a 50 kW transmitter from the Indian government, the radio artists secretly set it up at an undisclosed location near the border.

Every day, the radio station played songs and recitations from the Holy Quran. They also held passionate discussions on the Muktijuddho from an Islamic point of view. A special programme that their audience looked forward to was the daily broadcast of the pre-recorded speeches of Sheikh Mujibur Rahman.

The Swadhin Betar Bangla soon became the second front of the liberation war of Bangladesh. The radio played a vital role in keeping up the morale of freedom fighters as well as East Bengali civilians during the war.

During Operation Jackpot, the station was instrumental in communicating the all-important cue for action, embedded in a chosen radio programme, to the naval commandos. On 14 August, the leaders of all three commando groups started up their transistor radios and tuned in to Akashvani, the West Bengal branch of the All India Radio.

Across the border, in Delhi, a similar transistor radio was playing the same station. This one was sitting on Kao's desk, with Kao and Nair seated on either side.

In Calcutta, the radio jockey checked the time and played the song.

'Amar putul ajke prothom jabe shoshur bari ...'[24]
(Our doll will go to her in-laws' house for the first time today)

This song was the first signal for the three groups. It was a warning signal, instructing the commandos to get ready for action. In other words, they had to proceed to their target ports and wait for the next message to carry out the attack. Accordingly, the teams covered the remaining ground that night, getting as close to the ports as possible.

The group headed by Abdul Wahed Chowdhury was tasked with hitting the Chittagong port. They found themselves crouching in dense bushes behind a Mukti Bahini safe house, while the driver of a passing Pakistani Army truck relieved himself on the road.

Chowdhury checked his watch impatiently as the driver strolled back to the truck, got inside and started the ignition and left without incident. Chowdhury pulled his radio out of his pack and switched it on

---

[24] Aminur Rahman, 'Operation Jackpot', defenceforumindia.com, 3 September 2012.

at the decided hour. The others looked on tensely as he fiddled with the controls until he found the right frequency.

'Ami tomay joto shuniyechilem gan ...'[25]

(I ask no reward for the songs I sing to you ...)

This second song was the action signal. It was their command for the attack.

Chowdhury snapped the radio off and raised his hand. They had been given the go ahead.

It was 16 August. At around 2 a.m., sixty commandos participated in the Chittagong operation. Quickly and silently, their boats rolled out and they sneaked into the port using the Intelligence provided by on-ground assets. Once inside, they worked fast, having rehearsed this sequence for what had seemed like a hundred times. There was a strong wind and a light drizzle. The commandos had to swim against the strong currents of the Karnaphuli River. When they reached the target ships after swimming six to seven feet underwater, they scraped the dirt off the vessels with a knife and attached limpet mines on every Pakistani Army ship till they ran out of mines. The instructors had taught them to identify the best spots to place the explosives so that the vessel would suffer maximum damage.

---

[25] Aminur Rahman, 'Operation Jackpot', defenceforumindia.com, 3 September 2012.

They were also shown how to set up separate charges on the cables so that the ships would come crashing down horizontally, further crippling the ports.

Timers were attached to the limpet mines. The commandos set the timers and began to swim to where the boats were tethered. Their orders were clear: Run like hell and don't look back. The mines detonated with a deafening sound before they could swim ashore, though. Orange sparks of fire rained into the water. However, they all managed to escape death. As they saw the ships explode, 'Joy Bangla' was all they said.

Assets stationed outside the ports relayed the success of all the attacks to R&AW. Kao and Nair, who had both been sitting on the edges of their chairs, leaned back slowly with relief.

Kao called the PMO and informed Haksar about the success of Operation Jackpot.

Through Operation Jackpot, India's bid to block the main waterways of East Pakistan was accomplished with four simultaneous attacks. Eleven ships that belonged to the Pakistani Army were destroyed in Chittagong with zero casualties. Following the attack, the East Pakistani ports were declared non-operational and unsafe for foreign ships as well. A large number of the ships that were destroyed had been manufactured in countries allied to Pakistan, such as the US and France.

Pakistan was now left with no quick means to enter their own territory in the East. Both the air routes and the waterways had been blocked by India.

The world would talk about this masterstroke in the days to come. The international media picked it up and indicated that West Pakistan was losing control over East Pakistan.

Operation Jackpot had managed to deliver a crushing blow to the Pakistani Army's pride.

It was, in the truest sense, an Intelligence operation.

Chapter II

False Flag

YAHYA KHAN GRITTED HIS TEETH IN FURY AS HE poured his third large peg of whisky over the ice cubes in his glass and leaned back on his couch.

Throughout the monsoon, India had supported the Bangladesh Liberation Army by orchestrating a range of covert operations through the Mukti Bahini. The attacks had been relentless, and he knew that East Pakistan was slipping through his hands.

Yahya Khan always dreamt of being a great warrior, a ruler whom the world would remember for ages to come. He had grown up on stories about Genghis Khan, a brutal but brilliant leader. Genghis Khan had used tyranny as a weapon. Yahya Khan sought to leave behind a similar legacy. What he wanted, more than anything, was to win East Pakistan. Now, his dream was crumbling before his very eyes.

All his efforts seemed to have been in vain. Yahya Khan knew he wasn't left with too many options. The storm inside his head continued to rage as he raised his glass to his lips. He had to come up with a plan.

Meanwhile, in India, Kao knew that the iron was hot; it was time to strike.

◻

The success of Operation Jackpot was followed up with an escalation of guerrilla activity at the border, using Intelligence passed on to India by assets planted deep inside East Pakistan. The Mukti Bahini and the Mujib Bahini also kept up their attacks in the heart of enemy territory; attacks that were planned using reports from these R&AW operatives.

By October 1971, India was prepared for war, while Pakistan was teetering on the edge. Gen. Manekshaw, who had six months ago put his foot down, saying that the army was not ready, reported to Gandhi that his boys were now fully equipped.

Gandhi and her foreign affairs minister Sardar Swaran Singh went on a whirlwind global tour. Their mission was to impress on the West the urgent need for international intervention to end the genocide in East Pakistan and arrest the flow of refugees into India. This was an attempt to plead with the world to help stop the inevitable—another Indo-Pak war. But even while her efforts to prevent a war were genuine, Indira Gandhi was astute enough to put the armed forces in India on stand-by in case the negotiations and interventions failed.

After careful strategising, troops were moved and stationed all along India's eastern borders; however, for the world, Gandhi kept up the narrative that the soldiers were being moved east to deal with the insurgency in Assam.

Gandhi had a series of meetings with Kao, P.N. Dhar, Manekshaw and Haksar to decide what their next step should be. Prithvi Nath Dhar, an economist, was head of Indira Gandhi's secretariat and one of her closest advisers at the time.

At the meeting, Dhar said, 'An offensive at this stage will invite intervention by the United Nations (UN). Pakistan is already crying itself hoarse and blaming India. I suggest we keep up the pressure on Pakistan and wait for them to lose patience first.'

'I'm inclined to agree with Mr Dhar,' Kao said. 'We cannot be seen as the aggressor, especially after having pushed Pakistan so hard to do the same themselves.'

'Never interrupt an enemy when they are making a mistake,' Haksar warned from his end of the table.

'Said the great P.N. Haksar?' Dhar asked with a genial smile.

'Said the great Napoleon Bonaparte,' Haksar replied.

Quoting Napoleon was fine, Kao thought on the drive back to his office, but if Pakistan did not do something soon, they would have to devise new methods to instigate them.

Meanwhile, he was now beginning to sense a new rumble in the ranks of the guerrilla force. At Tajuddin Sheikh's request, the restriction on recruitment into the Mukti Bahini was eased out to accommodate soldiers of all political leanings. This was done so that its ranks could swell and help the war effort. This move had managed to pacify the grumblings from the soldiers of the Mukti and the other Bahinis against the Mujib Bahini, but it had also set a clock ticking. The war had to start before the radical members of the Bangladesh Liberation Army got overly influenced by the Maoist school of thought.

But Kao did not have to wait very long. What he hoped for, took place.

◻

On 19 November 1971, Pakistan took the bait. It was, by all means, a serious incident that provoked it.

A mixed battalion of Mukti Bahini and Indian Army soldiers had come face to face with the Pakistani Army in the village of Boyra in East Pakistan. The Indian troops had been covertly aiding the Mukti Bahini to capture areas in Garibpur, on the banks of the Brahmaputra River, about thirty kilometres from Boyra, but a chance skirmish with Pakistani border patrol forces exposed their mission. To counter the Indian troops, the Pakistani Army came rushing in, but was pounded by Indian tanks.

To support their troops, the PAF sent three fighter aircraft to provide air cover. All three were shot down by four Indian planes, but during this exchange, Pakistan ended up crossing into the Indian airspace several times, giving India an official reason to respond.

Using this pretext, India sanctioned a full-fledged offensive behind enemy lines as a response to the violation by the PAF. Pakistan stated that the violation had happened because Indian troops had crossed the border in the first place, but that was something Pakistan had been saying for months, and the world was tired of hearing it.

By 21 November, it was clear to everyone that matters had escalated. Kao, Dhar and Haksar were getting ready for a full-blown war.

❑

'The audacity,' Yahya Khan muttered under his breath, slamming his glass on the table. 'The bloody audacity.'

He was thinking of the speech Indira Gandhi had given in the Indian Parliament on 24 November, three days after the attack, a recording of which was later played on the news.

With a straight face, Indira Gandhi had said, 'It has never been our intention to escalate the situation.

We have instructed our troops not to cross the border except in self-defence. As for Pakistan's claims about us being engaged in an undeclared war with them, this is only propaganda and wholly untrue.'[26]

Yahya Khan was furious. India had gone too far. Now he was ready to go for the kill.

◻

'Yahya Khan is going to declare war in ten days,' Kao informed Sankaran Nair.

Kao had just returned from an emergency meeting in Gandhi's office. Earlier in the morning, she had received a call from foreign secretary T.N. Kaul, who had some interesting information to share.

'Find out what you can immediately about an American journalist named Bob Shapley. He works for *The New Yorker*,' Kao told Nair.

The previous day, Shapley had met Yahya Khan at a party in Pakistan, and the two men had got into a conversation. Predictably, Yahya Khan was soon inebriated and offered Shapley a ride on his way out. Shapley accepted, and in the car, asked the president if he could see him again in ten days for an interview.

'According to Kaul saab, Yahya Khan's exact words were that he would be at the front in ten days,' Kao said.

---

[26] Srinath Raghavan, *1971: A Global History of the Creation of Bangladesh* (Harvard University Press, Massachusetts, 2013), p. 232.

'And how does T.N. Kaul know this?' Nair countered.

'Shapley told the US Ambassador to India, Kenneth Keating, about the conversation. And Mr Keating thought it prudent to pass the information on to Kaul.'

Nair nodded. 'Which is why our first step should be to check out Shapley's credentials.'

'Yes,' Kao replied. 'It could be an attempt at misinformation on the part of Pakistan, but …'

'… but Yahya Khan is too much of a drunk to be able to pull that off?' Nair asked.

Kao chuckled. 'Even if he was acting on someone's advice, saying those exact words would be a new feat for him.'

'Assuming Shapley is kosher,' Nair asked, 'why would the head of a country go to the front?'

'Why indeed?' Kao said.

The work of verifying the Shapley tip-off began within the hour. The matter was sensitive and had to be handled with tact. The US and Pakistan were allies, and any information originating from the US had to be corroborated. However, Nair used his good offices and reached out to some credible sources in the CIA. He requested assistance in verifying Shapley's information. The R&AW spy network in Pakistan was activated as well. Nair reached out to his mole there with urgent demands for fresh Intelligence.

Simultaneously, the Mukti Bahini was contacted and instructed to go deep into East Pakistan to check for movement of troops.

'How is that satellite surveillance unit of yours working?' Kao asked M.B.K. Nair.

'It's working as well as it usually does. Why?'

'We'll need verification of whatever Intel the Mukti Bahini brings in.'

'I'll see to it myself,' M.B.K. Nair volunteered. 'Put my best boys on the job.' He turned to go, but then turned around again. 'What do you think they're planning?' he asked.

'Khan has been pushed against the wall,' Kao said. 'My guess is that he is going to come for us, all guns blazing.'

They were at the end of November. But both Kao and Nair knew that the ideal moment for Pakistan to strike would have been immediately after the battle at Boyra in mid-November. Indira Gandhi had already given her generals the go-ahead to exert pressure on East Pakistan's periphery with probing military actions to instigate a war. The entire machinery of the Indian armed forces had been poised for a declaration of war from Pakistan in mid-November.

It never came. Yahya Khan, in his infinite wisdom, let the moment pass, hoping that the UN would intervene. They didn't, and he lost the momentum that any other leader would have capitalised on, choosing instead to brood in his room while sipping whisky on the rocks.

Kao knew that every second Yahya Khan wasted was a boon for India. For his part, he made sure that India did not lose a single moment. Intelligence reports from all over were scanned, investigated and verified as fast as humanly possible.

R&AW operatives from Peshawar reported the movement of Pakistan's 7th Infantry Division towards the Poonch and Chhamb areas of the western Indian sector. In East Pakistan, R&AW agents in Dhaka and other major cities sent invaluable information concerning military installations in the region and their movements. This verified Intel was then passed on to the Indian Army and other branches of the armed forces so that they could plan their strategy in advance and prepare to counter the enemy's moves.

Manekshaw had the Army fully mobilised and ready.

Meanwhile, another team was set up to reap the benefits of what Sankaran Nair regarded to be his best achievement yet. He had, through the patience and doggedness of a deep-cover agent in West Pakistan, managed to install a tap on Yahya Khan's office phone.

It was a massive feat, and the team listening in on Yahya Khan's conversations knew better than to ask how it had been accomplished. There were whispers in R&AW that Nair had managed to turn one of Khan's domestic servants; others said that he had cultivated a source in the telephone exchange.

Nair had always been territorial about his sources. They were his best diamonds, the ones he couldn't afford to lose.

◻

By the end of November, there was no doubt in anyone's mind that Pakistan was preparing for war. The Mukti Bahini had reported massive movement of troops just beyond the border, much like India's deployment of troops months earlier. Satellite surveillance had confirmed the reports.

'But what are they going to do?' Nair wondered. 'How is it all going to start?'

Kao and Nair were tired. They had both been working almost non-stop for the last few days, and neither of them was getting any younger. The tap on Yahya Khan's phone was yielding only sporadic results, with hardly any new information coming in. They knew that Gen. Niazi was trying to impress upon the president the fact that decisive action was needed. The morale of the Pakistani soldiers was low. Bombarded by guerrilla warfare over several long months, they were retaliating without a concrete end in sight.

Despite his exhaustion, Kao knew that espionage was essentially a game of patience; they would have to wait to strike gold.

This time, they didn't have to wait too long. Nair's source in Karachi reached out to R&AW through his clandestine wireless set. In Morse code, he transmitted a message: 'Blitzkrieg without tanks. Khan is preparing to go to war by December 1.'

This was the confirmation they had been waiting for. But they wondered what the rest of the message meant.

'Like the Israeli air blitz,' Kao deduced.

He saw a look of confusion on the junior R&AW officers' faces.

'The Israeli Air Force carried out a pre-emptive strike against the Egyptian and Arab air forces, named Operation Focus, during the Six-Day War of 1967. They caught the enemy by surprise and got the upper hand in the war.'

Kao paused for a moment. 'They're going to launch airstrikes,' he continued. 'That's going to be the trigger.'

'Can we be sure about this?' Nair asked.

Kao shrugged. 'That's our best guess right now.'

There was a deathly silence in the room. D-Day was upon them.

□

The transcript of the call and the contents of the message from Nair's source were shared with Indira Gandhi and no one else.

She issued direct orders to move all aircraft from Indian Air Force (IAF) bases in the west and the north to safe locations. Gandhi was shrewd enough to anticipate Yahya Khan's plan. The egoistic Khan would act on the western sector with trademark Pakistani pre-emptive strikes which would grant legitimacy to a full-fledged counter-attack in East Pakistan. By attacking the west first, Yahya Khan was also hoping to relieve pressure in East Pakistan and to buy time for international action to reduce the intensity of the ongoing attacks in the east.

Overnight, every aircraft was moved into hardened shelters well away from the potential targets. If there was a direct attack, only the shelters would get damaged.

The entire armed forces machinery was placed on alert. The soldiers who were on pre-sanctioned leave were recalled with immediate effect. Granting of fresh leaves had been suspended weeks ago. Everyone was ordered to be ready to deploy at a moment's notice. Targets were assigned, routes were chalked out, and emergency contingency measures were discussed. Mukti Bahini units were instructed to continue their guerrilla warfare as if they knew nothing about the upcoming war.

By 1 December 1971, orders had been issued, and repeated over and over. By 2 December, India was ready for war. The troops were in place. Gandhi had already reached Calcutta in order to be closer to the action when the war began. The key players waited with bated breath.

The day passed without incident.

Chapter 12

An Incursion

KAO WAS EXHAUSTED. THE VIGIL THAT BEGAN ON THE night of 1 December 1971 had gone on for two days. It was 3 December, and the enemy still hadn't made their move. The spine-tingling anticipation had tied everyone's nerves in knots.

The hardest part of any Intelligence operation is the waiting, and this was, without dispute, the most significant operation that the agency had ever been involved in. Over six months, R&AW, along with the country's armed forces, had done everything in their power to provoke Pakistan to attack. All reports confirmed that Pakistan had taken the bait.

But now everyone at R&AW had the same question: 'Had they really?'

The IAF reached out to Nair. They were concerned that the pilots at the fighter bases of Adampur and Halwara had been sitting in the cockpit for the last forty-eight hours. They wanted to dismount them.

'Let's wait another twenty-four hours,' Nair countered. 'We will call off the vigil by 4 December, if nothing happens.'

At 5.40 p.m., on 3 December, the PAF made its first strike. Yahya Khan had decided to launch the surprise attack on a Friday, the auspicious Jumma day for Muslims. The time chosen was right after the evening prayers and also coincided with the change of shifts at the IAF base that was targeted.

Kao announced, 'The deed is finally done. Yahya Khan has made the first move; just got a message from the IAF base in Pathankot.'

Reports indicated that two Mirage IIIs (a reconnaissance craft and a strike escort) and a six-plane wing of F-86 Sabres flew towards the Pathankot Airbase. They dropped their first bomb on the runway. Five minutes later, four Mirages attacked the Amritsar Airbase with two 500 kg bombs.

As they continued their attacks at Pathankot and Amritsar with unguided rockets and bombs, subsequent strikes were directed at Ambala, Agra and Halwara at around 6 p.m. The PAF proceeded to deploy single or two-plane formations through the evening until 10.30 p.m. Airfields at Srinagar, Avantipur and Faridkot too were attacked. They carried out a total of sixteen air raids that night.

The operation was called Genghis Khan. Inspired by his warrior role-model, Yahya Khan intended to wage major wars on two fronts simultaneously and conquer East Pakistan in the process.

With infinite confidence, Yahya Khan had declared that he would catch the IAF napping and destroy them. He had even stated that he would seize Delhi by the next morning. Yahya Khan had launched a Pakistani version of Israel's 1967 Air Blitz, in hopes that one rapid attack would cripple India's far superior airpower.

On the morning of 4 December, Pakistan mounted eighteen more raids. Thus ended their 'pre-emptive' strike. India was now officially at war. All the plans and strategies that they had worked on for so many months would now be executed. It would all have to function like well-oiled machinery.

And Kao and Nair would have to play their part in making this happen.

❑

Pakistan mistook their small initial victory as a significant breakthrough. They thought they could easily 'knock the hell out of' the Indian Army. They didn't realise that the airbases had already been cleared out based on the Intel received by R&AW, and hence the damage had been minimal. And with Pakistan attacking first, India now had the perfect opportunity to go to war without looking like the aggressor.

Indira Gandhi left for Delhi from Calcutta immediately. She was travelling with Haksar. Sitting across the aisle, he voiced out loud what Gandhi was thinking to herself. 'The idiot has done exactly what we thought he would.'

In short, India was perfectly poised to occupy the moral high ground and press ahead into East Pakistan.

Gandhi landed in Delhi that night and was received by Swaran Singh. She drove straight to Army Headquarters to meet Gen. Manekshaw. He briefed her on the action on the western front. He also presented the plan for operations in the east and asked for her permission to launch the attacks. Gandhi looked Manekshaw squarely in the eye and asked him to hit Pakistan with everything that India had.

The press had been waiting for her arrival at 10 Janpath. In a measured voice, Gandhi said to them, 'War has been forced upon us.'[27]

On 4 December, the IAF flew more than 500 sorties, focused on tactical and strategic targets in Pakistan. By the evening that day, India had virtual air superiority in the western theatre of war.

In the fourteen days of war that followed, the Western Air Command of the IAF alone flew over 4,000 sorties. The IAF claimed ninety-four aircraft, while the PAF claimed eighty-one. This air campaign

---

[27] Rasheed Kidwai, 'How the 1971 War was Fought and Won', https://www. orfonline.org/research/how-1971-war-fought-won/, (2 February 2019).

demonstrated the value of mass and boldness. The IAF influenced the war significantly, with relatively smaller losses, while the PAF flew fewer sorties and had hardly any impact, but suffered higher losses.

Although China had provided Pakistan with military supplies, it remained unequal to India in military capacities. India had already developed an arms industry largely with the help of the Soviet Union. It was capable of producing major weapons such as the Vijayanta main battle tank and the HF-Marut fighter aircraft. As the war progressed, India continued to have access to military equipment from Moscow.

On the eastern front, the Indian forces responded with a massive and coordinated air, sea and land assault on the West Pakistani Army in East Pakistan. The IAF damaged the Dhaka airfield, the only one in the region, on 6 December 1971. The IAF now enjoyed total air superiority and the Mitro Bahini was able to take full advantage of India's domination of the airspace over East Bengal.

The Mitro Bahini was a new force that combined the strength of the Indian Army and the Mukti Bahini. Their orders were to charge into East Pakistani territory and hit with all their might. The Mitro Bahini fused guerrilla and tactical warfare to cause sustained damage to the Pakistani Army.

◻

From his office in Delhi, Kao strategised with Brig. Sujan Singh Uban of the SFF. The force had been placed under the direct command of the R&AW for missions precisely like the one Kao was now telling Uban to execute.

'Uban, sabotage and harass them. Get into their heads. Destroy what you can. Bring back the Chittagong Hill Tracts.'

Uban mounted Operation Eagle in the Chittagong Hills. It was an extremely secret mission, known only to R&AW and the SFF. No official records exist of this operation.

Throughout the 1971 war, Uban's Tibetan forces kept up an aggressive campaign of sabotage and harassment. They succeeded in destroying several vital bridges and ensuring that Pakistan's 97 Independent Brigade and crack 2 Commando Battalion remained pressured in the Hill Tracts. The SFF functioned at an optimal rate with only 56 dead and 190 wounded.

While R&AW and the Indian Army strategised their moves in India, Yahya Khan seemed to be whiling away his time in Karachi. It was reported that Khan was making the legendary Pakistani singer Noor Jehan sing for him on long-distance phone calls from Japan. As she crooned beautiful songs to the president, Yahya Khan would interrupt to shower praises on her. A war had broken out, but Yahya Khan had chosen to cocoon himself in the company of women and wine rather than lead his men in the war that he had begun.

To his surprise, Kao observed that the Pakistan Army was every bit as self-assured as Yahya Khan. When the pre-emptive strikes were launched, the chief of PAF told the military's public relations (PR) officer not to bother conjuring up a justification. 'Success is the biggest justification,' the PAF chief had boasted. 'My bird should be right over Agra by now, knocking the hell out of them. I am only waiting for the good news.'[28]

'Hardly surprising,' Nair observed. 'Their vulnerability is coupled with curious overconfidence about their superiority vis-à-vis India. The idea of the innate superiority of the Muslim soldier was bequeathed to Pakistan by the British Raj's theory of martial races. You know, the idea that one Muslim warrior is worth ten Hindus. It has since then been internalised by its military classes.'

But Pakistan's war strategies were all backfiring, and with good reason. Earlier in the year, Pakistan had purged the Bengali units from the army. Many Bengalis, especially those who belonged to the West Pakistan units, had defected, and those who remained were not trustworthy. Consequently, the combat

---

[28] Srinath Raghavan, *1971: A Global History of the Creation of Bangladesh* (Harvard University Press, Massachusetts, 2013), pp. 231–34.

effectiveness of the units suffered, especially that of the PAF, as a majority of the ground crew had been Bengali. The Pakistani military services were also weakened by the fact that they had been politicised. The structure of the army was overly centralised, as Yahya Khan had wanted to retain his control over its operations in addition to his duties as president and supreme commander of Pakistan's armed forces. Communications and cooperation between the three forces of the Pakistani Army—located in Rawalpindi, Peshawar and Karachi—suffered as a result.

There was no doubt that the Pakistani Army had lost its original vigour. And, India was capitalising on their dwindling alertness and strength.

□

Three days after the war began, on 6 December 1971, Gandhi publicly recognised Bangladesh as an independent state. The declaration had been a long time coming. But it had been imperative for India to keep her position a secret until the war had begun. Gandhi was prudent enough to first secure empathy from the UN and world media for choosing to participate in the war before revealing where India's sympathies lay.

There was some international blowback, of course. Nixon was upset and told Kissinger that he had warned Indira Gandhi to not take action against Pakistan. Nixon and Kissinger set out to mobilise help for Pakistan from France, China and a few West Asian countries, asking them to send their fighter aircraft to help Pakistan in the war. The Chinese chose not to react to the message. It was then that Nixon knew Pakistan was fighting a losing battle.

Many months after the war had ended, Maj. Gen. Sukhwant Singh, who was the deputy director of military operations in 1971, made an interesting observation which had great strategic relevance for Pakistan: 'The tactical imbalance of the Indian Army which existed because of the improper locations of troops was redressed by the third week of October. Yahya waited too long to go to war in December. By this time, the Indian Army was well prepared to tackle the Pakistan offensive, and Yahya lost the strategic advantage of a pre-emptive attack. The best time for Pakistan would have been to launch an offensive operation in October.'[29]

These were observations and lessons that Pakistan would study and analyse for months and years after the war ended. Without strong leadership, Pakistan's armed forces ended up fighting a defensive battle, devoid of strategy, both on land and in the air.

[29] Sukhwant Singh, *India's Wars Since Independence: The Liberation of Bangladesh* (Vikas Publishing House, New Delhi, 1991), p. 49.

However, their naval prowess, especially the Karachi port, was Pakistan's pride—something they counted on as their trump card for winning the war. India knew this too. They had to find a way to obstruct Pakistan's access to the seas.

Chapter 13

In Enemy Waters

THREE INDIAN NAVY MISSILE BOATS, ARMED TO THE teeth, were in the Arabian Sea, speeding north to attack the Karachi harbour. Suddenly, en route, the radar on one of the boats started beeping. An enemy warship had been spotted. PNS *Khaibar* was approaching the missile boat and was at a distance of 120 kilometres. The Indian boat had been discovered, and its captain knew it was just a matter of time before they would be attacked. They were in enemy waters, after all. The captain knew he had to make a move quickly. It was his only chance. He took aim and launched the anti-ship missile towards PNS *Khaibar*.

This was Trident, India's secret naval operation, which was now in its final stages. The date was 5 December 1971.

Interestingly, this operation had its genesis a couple of months ago in an adventure involving two fictional-sounding characters—Rod and Moriarty. They were two R&AW operatives who had undertaken a perilous journey by sea into the Karachi harbour.

In October 1971, approximately two months before the war had begun, a meeting was held at which defence minister Jagjivan Ram, chief of the Indian Navy S.M. Nanda, and Kao were present. The Indian Navy had received information that Karachi port had recently installed the latest naval surveillance equipment available. The naval commander asked Kao if he could investigate and verify the information.

Kao knew that they would need substantial visual documentation to study and gauge the quality of Pakistan's naval surveillance technology. This kind of information-gathering was not a task for their foot soldiers. They needed expert spymasters to look into the matter.

So Kao and Nair came up with a plan.

Nair contacted his top agent in Bombay and told him what he required. Five days later, the agent called back, saying that he had a plan and knew a person who could help them out. Nair flew down to Bombay himself to set the plan in motion.

'The person who can help us is Cowasji Doctor,' the Bombay agent said. 'He is a Parsi doctor who shuttles between India and Pakistan via Kuwait on his ship. It's not a very big one, but it has a sickbay.'

'Okay, but can we trust him?'

'Frankly, I don't know for sure. But there is something which we can use to our advantage.' The agent slid a file across the table for Nair to read.

Two months earlier, Cowasji Doctor had been caught bringing in expensive undeclared goods on his ship. He now faced an enquiry by the Customs department. The investigation was still underway and would most likely result in a hefty fine, putting a dent in the good doctor's finances.

Nair knew what needed to be done. The chief of Bombay Customs was a friend of his. He picked up the phone and dialled his number. After they had exchanged a few pleasantries, Nair told his friend about his problem. Ten minutes later, the deal was struck. The R&AW, from their secret fund, would pay the fine on Doctor's behalf, and the Customs department would issue a letter declaring the matter closed. The letter, however, would be hand-delivered to Nair and not to Cowasji Doctor.

Armed with the letter, Nair, accompanied by two trusted R&AW agents, visited the doctor at his clinic on D.N. Road in south Bombay, introducing himself as Commander Menon with the Indian Navy.

'This letter can be yours if you help us out with a small task. You can refuse, of course, but if you do, I'm under orders to burn this letter, and the enquiry against you will be reopened.'

Doctor realised that the choice he was being offered was no choice at all.

'What do you need?' he asked.

'You will be taking two men with you on your next trip to Pakistan. The trip will have to start within the next two days. I'm sure you'll find a good reason,' Nair said, smiling.

Doctor nodded, and Nair stood up to leave.

'At least tell me who I'm taking with me,' Doctor said.

'All you need to know is this. Their names are Rod and Moriarty.'

Their real names were Rao and Murty. Rao was Nair's naval assistant, and Murty was the R&AW specialist from the photography department.

□

The mission was undertaken in October 1971, well before the conflict had officially begun. However, India knew that war with Pakistan was unavoidable. Before Pakistan decided to strike, India had to gather as much information as possible about its naval forces. Time, as the expression goes, was of the essence.

R&AW was getting Intel about the US's secret supply of weapons and defence equipment to Pakistan. It also knew that, in the event of war, the Karachi port would be the Pakistani Navy's most valuable base and asset. The only way India could gain the upper hand in the naval fight was by knowing exactly what Pakistan's ship strength was, and by being able to gauge its offensive and defensive capabilities.

After the meeting with 'Commander Menon', as planned, Doctor set sail two days later, with two new members aboard—Rod and Moriarty. The trip was uneventful until the ship entered Pakistani waters. As they had expected, in light of the heightened tensions between the two countries, every vessel entering Pakistani territory was being strictly screened for any suspicious cargo or activity. By this time, Pakistan had also become aware of a new Intelligence agency in India which was capable of running the most audacious and devious missions. They didn't know the official name of this secret organisation yet.

Cowasji Doctor's ship docked at the Karachi harbour. Before Doctor could even look over the railings, an inspector with Pakistan's Criminal Investigation Department (CID) came aboard with two of his subordinate officers. Doctor was extremely nervous. His heart was in his mouth as the officers went over the relevant papers. Within minutes, the inspector's team had gone over the ship and confirmed that two of the passengers mentioned in the manifest were not in their berths. The men were hiding as they didn't want to be seen by the inspector.

'Rod and Moria … Moriarty?' Reading the names out from the ship's manifest, the inspector looked suspiciously at Doctor. 'Where are they?'

The nervous doctor looked at the inspector and his men who were waiting for him to answer. He knew he had to save himself.

'Oh, yes! I know what you must be thinking. Strange names. You know … Indian Christians … they have all sorts of names,' Doctor rambled. 'They are in the sickbay. Fell ill rather suddenly, you see.'

'Go check the sickbay,' the inspector snapped to one of his officers.

'Oh, I wouldn't recommend that … I wouldn't recommend that. They're both down with chickenpox, you see. One of them contracted it and passed it on to the other. The entire sickbay is off-limits for the rest of us till they get well. It was the only place where I could isolate them.'

The inspector and his junior officers took what Doctor had said at face value. The man had been making regular trips to Karachi for years, and they had never had any reason to suspect him. They let the ship enter the harbour.

A relieved Doctor waited for the CID officers to disappear. Then he went inside to fix himself a stiff scotch and soda. He needed it.

At midnight, the ship set sail again and was navigated carefully to a pre-decided spot between two cliffs at the entry point of the harbour. Rod and Moriarty were ready with their cameras, peeping through the portholes.

'Are you seeing this?' Rod asked, amazed at the sight in front of him.

'It's magnificent,' Moriarty answered, equally awestruck.

They looked at each other and then again at the object in front of them.

'Looks like it was recently erected,' Rod said.

It was a newly built structure on which an anti-aircraft battery was mounted. This meant that Pakistan was readying the port for war.

Working quickly, the agents clicked photographs by the dozen, zooming in as tightly as the lens allowed, so as to capture the precise positions of all the fortifications and gun mountings. But most importantly, they managed to photograph some of the navy ships which were moored at the port.

Nearly thirty minutes had elapsed before the sweating pilot was told he could turn back. Then Rod and Moriarty headed back to the sickbay where they remained the next day, while Doctor, for the sake of appearances, made a few visits and then returned to the vessel in the afternoon. The ship then set off from Karachi. As it sailed out of the harbour, the two agents photographed the other side of the cliff as well.

The ship then entered the Arabian Sea and headed for Kuwait. There, Rao and Murty got off and made straight for the Indian Embassy. The undeveloped film rolls that they carried were flown to Delhi on a priority basis. Rao and Murty flew to India the next day.

In Delhi, two photographers were already waiting in a fully equipped laboratory where the films were delivered to them. By the next morning, a thick stack of photographs in an envelope with 'URGENT' emblazoned across it was resting atop the pile of papers on Jagjivan Ram's desk.

In the war room, Ram, Kao and Nanda studied the photographs. Murty took them through the images, giving them a 360-degree view of the harbour. Everyone looked at the material in front of them with astonishment and admiration.

For the first time, India had visuals from the inside of the Karachi port. The Indian Navy now knew where the defensive structures were and what their capability was. They knew the exact locations of the fuel storage facility and the naval ship moorings. They were now in an advantageous position to plan their operations.

India had stripped Pakistan's Naval Intelligence bare.

❑

By the time war was officially declared on 3 December 1971, the Indian Navy had a detailed inventory of the defences of Karachi harbour.

At the time, the Indian Navy had the aircraft carrier INS *Vikrant*, three destroyers, two cruisers, fourteen frigates, six missile boats and four submarines.

Pakistan's naval power was, at best, quite modest, concentrated in a single major naval base in Karachi. They had placed their best men on their newly acquired Dolphin Class submarines. Only 5,000 of their 8,000 navy personnel were deployed in the war. The reduced effective strength was a result of the military operation in East Pakistan in March, earlier that year. The force was further depleted in number by the time the war began, as the Bengali personnel had either deserted or were no longer trusted by the Pakistani Navy.

The Pakistani Navy, already at a disadvantage, was further crippled by their leader Yahya Khan's furious and completely short-sighted actions. Yahya Khan was so whimsical, the Pakistani Naval Chief did not know about the president's plan to go to war until 29 November 1971. And he found out that war had broken out only through the news on the radio. All these factors worked to Pakistan's disadvantage and their naval strategy in the war, of necessity, had to be a defensive one. Hence, the Pakistani Navy aimed to avoid direct battle with Indian Navy surface ships and concentrate on safeguarding its coastline.

On the night of 3 December 1971, when India declared war on Pakistan, the Indian Navy was already planning to go on the offensive, starting with a mission bound for the Karachi harbour. The plan was set in motion on 4 December.

It began with the IAF bombing Karachi and the airports at Mahir and Badin near the city. Indian fighter planes also kept strafing the environs of the Karachi harbour, showering rockets continuously. The air action was actually a ploy to divert Pakistan's attention from the combat fleets that were approaching Karachi waters that night with specific missions in their sights.

The Indian Navy had acquired Osa-I missile boats from the Soviet Union in early 1971. These were deadly boats that could strike deep and destroy big cruisers. Indian naval commanders realised that they could be instrumental during the war. But they had a major disadvantage: these missile boats were designed primarily for coastal defence and had a short striking range. However, the naval commanders wanted to use these boats for an attack. They came up with the audacious idea of towing the boats from Mumbai to a point within striking distance of Karachi harbour.

Thus, an ingenious manoeuvre was initiated in tandem with the IAF. As the IAF kept the pressure up on Karachi through constant attacks, three Osa-I missile boats furtively made their way to Karachi from Mumbai. Their mission was the ultimate destruction of the Karachi harbour. This was Operation Trident.

The three Indian missile boats were successfully towed very close to Pakistani waters and released around 250 nautical miles off the Karachi harbour. The boats were steaming ahead at full speed when one of their radars started beeping—an enemy ship was approaching. The Indian boat's captain made a quick decision and fired a missile towards the ship. Minutes later, the approaching Pakistani ship was hit. A second missile was fired, which managed to sink the Pakistani vessel. It was the PNS *Khaibar*, one of the Pakistani Navy's most potent ships.

But the horror was just beginning for Pakistan. They were unable to comprehend what had hit the ship. They mistook the Styx missiles from the Osa-I to be an attack from the IAF. Then, before they could even recover from the loss of PNS *Khaibar*, the second Indian missile boat damaged a destroyer and a cargo ship which was carrying ammunition for the Pakistani forces. The third boat of the 'Trident' formation attacked the Karachi harbour. It was a targeted, three-pronged attack, planned with the help of the visual Intel provided by Rao and Murty. It managed to destroy the fuel storage facility at the Karachi harbour completely.

The first-ever missile attack launched on the Karachi harbour was concluded on the morning of 5 December. It was a great success as it had dealt a significant blow to the Pakistani Navy's fighting capabilities. The resulting fuel shortage and the Indian Navy's superior striking capabilities forced the Pakistan Navy to withdraw its surface combatants into its protected harbour.

But even after this crippling blow, Pakistan continued to receive war supplies from its friends abroad. This, too, had to be stopped.

A subsequent mission was mounted, complementing Operation Trident. It was called Operation Python. Operation Python's goal was to create a naval blockade around Karachi port. This second Indian naval raid was executed on the night of 8 December 1971, and it inflicted additional destruction on Pakistan's shore installations in Karachi and left a Navy oiler, PNS *Dacca*, damaged.

The triumph of Operation Trident and Operation Python effectively accomplished the naval blockade of Pakistan. The purpose of the blockade was to isolate West Pakistan from East Pakistan completely. India now dominated the air and the waters in the theatre of war. This meant that there was no possibility of Pakistan either reinforcing or withdrawing its armed forces in East Pakistan. Furthermore, the successive attacks demoralised the Pakistani forces, leaving them confused about the nature and strength of their attackers.

The Pakistan Navy attempted to hit back at the
Indian Navy. It was able to strike below the waves, with
a Daphné-class submarine called PNS *Hangor*. PNS
Hangor managed to sink an Indian ship, INS *Khukri*,
on 9 December. INS *Khukri* was an anti-submarine
frigate. She was torpedoed thrice in quick succession,
and sank with its captain, seventeen officers and 176
sailors on board. It was the only ship that India lost
during the war. The Indian Navy was able to rescue six
officers, and sixty-one sailors survived the attack.

◻

While the Indian Navy was successfully attacking the
Pakistani Navy on the western shores, a different kind
of drama was unfolding in eastern waters in the Bay
of Bengal.

The pride of the Pakistani Navy, the submarine PNS
Ghazi, had slipped out of Karachi harbour sometime
between 14 and 20 November. American-built and
complemented with strong weapons, PNS *Ghazi* was
the only ship in the Pakistani inventory that the Indian
Navy was wary of. Being a submarine, she was also
hard to detect and thus posed a significant challenge
to the Indian Navy's ships.

R&AW's spies had noted the departure of *Ghazi*
from Karachi and immediately informed the Indian
Navy about it. They also deduced correctly that *Ghazi*

would make her way to the Bay of Bengal, and that her target would be INS *Vikrant*.

At 19,500 tons, INS *Vikrant* was the Indian Navy's largest ship. It could carry around twenty-three fighter aircraft to attack distant targets. Sinking or even disabling *Vikrant* would be a massive blow to Indian naval power, undermining India's war effort. India knew that Pakistan was aware of this fact as well.

To counter Pakistan's submarine offensive, the Indian Navy started laying a trap for PNS *Ghazi*.

The Indian Navy destroyer INS *Rajput* was selected to be a decoy for INS *Vikrant*. From the waters of Visakhapatnam, INS *Rajput* started sending across demands for rations, fuel and other materials—in quantities suggestive of large ships such as INS *Vikrant*. In addition to these demands, INS *Rajput* also started sending and receiving heavy wireless traffic, comparable to that of *Vikrant*. *Rajput* did this on open channels, hoping that PNS *Ghazi* would pick up the signals while prowling around the Bay of Bengal, and fall for the trick.

India also trusted that Pakistani spies operating in the area would relay the location of the faux *Vikrant* to the Pakistani authorities. They kept up the drama for days.

On the night of 3 December 1971, INS *Rajput* was instructed to sail out of Visakhapatnam. The

Indian authorities were now sure that PNS *Ghazi* was very close to Visakhapatnam, waiting for what she thought was INS *Vikrant*. And sure enough, the Indian deception had worked! *Ghazi* had latched on to all the false signals and information sent out by *Rajput* and was waiting to pounce on her prey.

But before she could lay her claws on INS *Rajput*, the tables were turned, and *Rajput*, in fact, discovered her location. *Ghazi* did her best to evade the Indian destroyer, but *Rajput* caught up with her and managed to sink her in a massive explosion.

During the course of this entire drama, the actual INS *Vikrant* was sailing safely on the East Pakistan coast, readying her aircraft to pound the Pakistani military on land.

Amid the wreckage of the sunken *Ghazi*, Indian divers later found a secret message: 'Intelligence indicates Carrier in port. Proceed to Visakhapatnam with all dispatch.'[30]

□

The war had been going on for some days, and India had achieved virtual air and naval superiority on both the eastern and western fronts. Prolonging the war would attract intervention from the UN and

---

[30] G.M. Hiranandani, *Transition to Triumph: Indian Navy 1956–1975* (Lancer Publishers, New Delhi, 2000), p. 142.

international pressure to end the conflict. However, India was yet to gain control of Dhaka. It was the only obstacle that remained on the path to achieving Bangladesh's freedom.

Chapter 14

Airdrop

SCORES OF CARGO PLANES, FLYING LOW, HOVERED over the land; it was as if they were floating in the air. Then the bellies of the planes opened, and one by one, the Indian paratroopers started dropping. On that breezy afternoon, Tangail in East Pakistan, a mere 98 kilometres from Dhaka, witnessed a spectacular feat. It seemed as if the south-eastern sky was covered with giant balloons, descending gently to the ground.

It was 11 December 1971. The Tangail airdrop had commenced.

The airdrop was the beginning of the climax of the war. Over the past week, the ground forces had been acting on express orders from Gen. Manekshaw, who was slowly turning up the pressure.

From 4 December onwards, Manekshaw, realising that all would be lost if the ceasefire resolution was passed in the UN, had kept up a steady barrage in order to pressurise Pakistani forces to surrender. An immediate ceasefire and withdrawal of troops would sabotage, perhaps forever, the Awami League's chances of forming a government headed by Sheikh Mujibur Rahman in East Bengal.

◻

On land, the Indian forces were fighting simultaneous battles with Pakistan on its western and eastern borders. The first major achievement during this phase of the war was the successful defence of the Longewala post by the 23 Punjab Regiment. Longewala is a border town in Rajasthan's Jaisalmer district.

The battle started at 1 a.m. on 5 December, when Pakistani troops began closing in around Longewala with two tank squadrons and two infantry companies. The attack continued for six hours. Indian defenders led by Maj. Kuldeep Singh Chandpuri, though vastly outnumbered and outgunned, managed to destroy several Pakistani tanks and hold their position.

At the break of dawn, the IAF mounted a series of attacks from the Jaisalmer airfield and destroyed three tanks in the first sortie. Another attack was launched at 9.30 a.m. and kept up till 11 a.m., when the Pakistani troops finally decided to cut their losses and withdraw. The IAF managed to retain the Longewala post, destroying seventeen Pakistani tanks and damaging twenty-three more.

While intermittent shelling continued in Longewala from 6 December, the company defending the post held out stubbornly, even advancing to capture Masit Wari-Bhit border on 10 December and Tamanchi Wala Toba on 11 December.

Another aggressive tank battle was waged in Basantar at the Shakargarh Bulge. The bulge was a protrusion of Pakistani territory into the Indian side. This particular spot was surrounded on three sides by India and was strategically important for both the countries. The road to Jammu from Punjab passed through this area. Pakistan hoped to launch a significant invasion into Shakargarh and take control of the route, completely cutting off road access to Jammu and Kashmir in order to put pressure on India. India fought back fiercely, in a battle that lasted twelve days. It was the biggest tank battle to be fought after World War II, and it ended with a victory for the Indian troops.

❑

Meanwhile, on the East Pakistan borders, due to vast stretches of marshy terrain and the absence of roads and tracks, the Indian Army's progress was steady but slow. The Pakistani Army had left the roads to Dhaka undefended, focusing on the bridgeheads and a few strong points. The tactic was to delay the Indian advance until the UN and international pressure intervened to put a stop to it.

On 6 December, the Indian troops pushed in from all sides towards Jessore, which lies 190 kilometres southwest of Dhaka, slowly tightening a noose around the retreating Pakistanis. Jessore was strategically very important—it was right in the heart of East Pakistan.

After a fierce 24-hour battle, Jessore was secured by the Indian Army. Its Pakistani defenders, around 5,000 men, fled in disarray to the south.

The victory at Jessore meant Indian forces now controlled about half of East Pakistan.

On the same day, another daredevil operation, headed by Gen. Sagat Singh, was carried out.

Gen. Sagat Singh and his troops wanted to join in the fight for Dhaka, but they were in Brahmanbaria, in east-central Bangladesh. To reach Dhaka, they would have to cross the mighty Meghna River. The only bridge over the river had been damaged, though. The troops were stuck, and time was ticking away.

It was then that Gen. Singh had a brainwave. He would arrange for his soldiers and the Mukti Bahini troops to be airlifted over the river. This would also mean that they could bypass the Pakistani Army on the other side. This was Operation Meghna Heli Bridge.

The operation was brilliantly conceived, but very risky. The Indian troops barely had enough ammunition and artillery to hold their own if attacked by the Pakistani Army. For tactical reasons, this operation would also have to be conducted under cover of darkness. That meant low visibility to enemy eyes, but it rendered the landing of the helicopters carrying the troops risky. But the motivated Indian forces were determined to take on the mission.

From 9 December to 11 December, over 36 hours, around 700 Indian soldiers were successfully heli-lifted in 110 sorties over the Meghna River. Once they had landed, the men fought the Pakistani troops with all their might and secured the eastern roads to Dhaka.

By 11 December, the war was drawing to a close. The combined strength of the Indian armed forces and the Mukti Bahini were steadily gaining the upper hand, and the Pakistani troops were beating a hasty retreat. All the effort that the R&AW had put into raising the Mukti Bahini was finally paying dividends. The guerrilla army had succeeded in penetrating deep into East Pakistan, and every day, there were reports of more and more ground being captured.

Now only one objective remained. Dhaka.

■

The Pakistani Army was stubbornly defending Dhaka, and it would have to be captured before the UN announced a ceasefire.

That is when the decision was taken to airdrop a battalion of soldiers directly into Dhaka, or as close to it as possible. And Tangail was chosen as the dropping point. Tangail is about 80 kilometres northwest of Dhaka. There were no river crossings between the two places, so the approach to Dhaka would be almost eventless. A successful landing of paratroopers in Tangail could be the final impetus needed to win Dhaka.

All preparations for the drop had already been set in motion by R&AW through Mukti Bahini. The guerrilla force, in order to express its gratitude for the victory that was now in plain sight, ensured that every requirement from R&AW was met post-haste.

This time, R&AW also had a real ace in the hole. They called him Tiger Siddiqui, and he was a legend among the rank and file, for good reason.

Tiger Siddiqui's real name was Abdul Kader Siddiqui. He had been a soldier in the Pakistani Army but voluntarily retired from military service before 1971 and returned to his hometown in Tangail. When Pakistani forces entered Tangail after Operation Searchlight, Siddiqui, like other local leaders, left town to escape arrest. But unlike the others, Siddiqui remained in East Pakistan and formed a guerrilla outfit—the Kader Bahini.

Siddiqui began to comb the rural areas to collect arms and recruits, and started organising a resistance force. Youths, labourers, students and professionals were among those who enthusiastically joined the Kader Bahini. Formally, it had been in operation since 21 April 1971, and at the time of the war, it comprised 17,000 fighters. Their operational area was spread over 1,500 square kilometres; 'Tiger' and his unit fought mostly in and around Tangail district, including Dhaka.

The Kader Bahini disrupted the Pakistan Army's progress by damaging their communication systems. They also snared army columns, struck military convoys, and blew up supply and ammunition dumps. By blowing up bridges, they managed to restrict the movements of the Pakistani Army in the district. Tiger Siddiqui and Kader Bahini had the support of R&AW. The agency regularly helped Tiger in his operations, and in turn he passed on information to R&AW. Kao had identified Tiger as a key player for the Tangail airdrop.

Another vital role in the operation was assigned by R&AW and the Indian Army to Dr Nuran Nabi. Nabi was a scientist turned freedom fighter who worked with the Mukti Bahini. He was chosen to act as liaison between Tiger, the Mukti Bahini and the Indian Army.

In Tangail, Dr Nabi met with a R&AW agent who only gave his name as Peter. Peter had arrived in Tangail the previous night along with five freedom fighters, three of whom were trained wireless set operators. Peter's mission was to contact Tiger Siddiqui and select strategic locations for the landing of the Indian paratroopers. Nabi was to take Peter to Tiger.

Nabi set up Peter's meeting with Tiger the next day. Tiger assured Nabi and Peter that they would have the complete support of the Kader Bahini for the Tangail airdrop. The preparations for the drop began.

On 7 December, Peter, Nabi and Tiger reached a pre-decided spot—an abandoned school where a camp had been set up. There were 150 freedom fighters at the camp to help the Indian Army achieve the ultimate objective: Dhaka.

Nabi was put in charge of communications for all subsequent attacks. His job was to coordinate between the different companies, maintain constant contact with Tiger, and help Peter in his work.

Just the previous day, on 6 December, Indira Gandhi had officially recognised Bangladesh as a free country. In Tangail, Tiger's presence coupled with the news of India's recognition of Bangladesh created a feverish excitement amongst the people. That evening, after the namaz, thousands of people assembled at the school ground where Tiger gave a passionate speech. Peter and Nabi were deeply impressed by the large turnout, as well as the support and enthusiasm they expressed. For the next three days, preparations progressed as planned for the airdrop and subsequent attacks.

D-Day for the Tangail airdrop was 11 December 1971.

At around 5 p.m., Nabi, in charge of communications, tuned his wireless set to the right frequency and broadcast a message to Tiger and other commanders in the area, only saying, 'They are coming.'

Not just soldiers, but the local people, too, were out in the open, waiting, when two IAF MiGs flew very low over Tangail. Even as people were trying to guess where exactly they would airdrop the battalion, the MIGs shot upwards, revealing cargo planes, which started descending. The MIGs were only conducting a reconnaissance foray.

In a glorious sight, a battalion of around 600 men was airdropped into Tangail. The sky was full of descending paratroopers and their supply drops. The locals cheered wildly and even helped retrieve and carry their ammunition for them.

In Delhi, the news of the airdrop reached Kao through Manekshaw. The first phase of their strategy was a resounding success.

The second phase was already in progress. The Mukti Bahini had captured all major roads connecting to Tangail. Now they were all set to seize the most important of them all—the Poongli bridge.

The Poongli bridge on the Jamuna River connected Mymensingh in the north to Dhaka. Intelligence reports had confirmed that the retreating Pakistani 93rd Brigade was approaching Dhaka via that bridge. The paratroopers dropped into Tangail were instructed to stall the retreat of the Pakistani troops. The paras commenced their attack. Within two hours, they succeeded in their mission.

The Tangail airdrop and the subsequent capture of the Poongli bridge gave the advancing Indian Army the manoeuvrability to sidestep the strongly held Tongi–Dhaka Road. They then captured the undefended Manikganj–Dhaka Road. The Indian Army was now on its way to Dhaka.

■

The Indian armed forces had no time to rejoice in their victory, though.

At the same time, a spectacle was being orchestrated on the waters of the Bay of Bengal. On 10 December 1971, R&AW intercepted an American message indicating that the US's Seventh Fleet was steaming into the war zone. The Seventh Fleet included a 75,000-ton nuclear-powered aircraft carrier, the USS *Enterprise*. It was the world's largest warship, and it carried more than seventy fighter planes and bombers. 'Officially', the US Seventh Fleet wanted to secure American citizens in Bangladesh, but unofficially it had been sent to help Pakistan win the war.

Standing between the Indian coast and the American ships was the Indian Navy's Eastern Fleet led by INS *Vikrant*, with barely twenty-three light fighter aircraft on board. India didn't stand a chance against the USS *Enterprise* by herself.

India had also received information from Soviet Intelligence that a British aircraft carrier, Eagle, had moved closer to India's territorial waters in the Arabian Sea.

It was ironic that Britain and the US, the world's two leading democracies, were uniting to fight India, the largest democracy. They had planned a coordinated pincer to help Pakistan, which had just perpetrated in Bangladesh the most massive genocide in history since the Holocaust.

However, India did not panic.

It quietly sent Moscow a request to activate a secret provision of the Indo-Soviet security treaty that was signed in August that year. Under this treaty, Russia was bound to defend India in case of any external aggression.

To counter this two-pronged British–American threat, Russia dispatched a nuclear-powered flotilla on 13 December. Though the Russian fleet comprised a good number of nuclear-armed ships and atomic submarines, their missiles were of limited range. Hence, to effectively take on the British and American navies, the Russian commanders had to undertake the risk of encircling the fleets to bring them within their target. And they did this with military precision.

With the Russians intervening like they meant business, the Americans and the British didn't follow through with their threat to India. Thus the Russian manoeuvre helped prevent a direct clash between India and the US–UK combine.

Once the possibility of a major clash on water had been averted, Manekshaw motivated his troops to get to Dhaka and end the war as soon as possible.

❑

In fact, one of the most critical consequences of the para-drop was yet to be played out.

Except for Peter and Tiger, no one on the ground knew the actual strength of the drop. Everyone guessed at the number, and this led to the classic Chinese whisper situation. Each time the information was passed on, the estimated number of paratroopers was inflated. It did not take too long for news of a major landing to reach Pakistani troops. R&AW communicated to the Indian Army's PR desk to take advantage of the Chinese whispers floating around the drop and publicise them widely.

A young and enthusiastic PR officer remembered an event in Agra from some time back. A large number of paratroopers had landed in the city from flying aircraft. The young officer found a photograph which showed the descent of a brigade of about 5,000 soldiers. On 12 December, the PR officer sent the photo from the Agra event, along with news of the Tangail airdrop, to all the leading international newspapers. Conveniently, he didn't mention in the accompanying press release that it was a 'file photo'. Only Kao was aware of what the PR officer had done. The officer, Rammohan Rao, later went on to join R&AW.

The photograph of the grand spectacle appeared in newspapers across the world. It had the effect that R&AW and the Indian Army had wished for. The world believed that a large brigade had been airdropped into Tangail and was on its way to capture Dhaka.

R&AW also intercepted a call between Gen. Niazi and Yahya Khan at the Pakistani Army's general headquarters. Call interception was in full force by then, and hundreds of calls were being monitored every hour. The recordings were sent to the concerned officers as fast as they could be; often there was simply too much data to disseminate.

In this particular call, a panicked Niazi was telling Yahya Khan that India had para-dropped a brigade of around 5,000 men in Tangail. The Chinese whispers, combined with the photograph, had done its job.

The information was a gross overstatement, as the Tangail battalion consisted of only about 500 to 600 soldiers. However, Niazi clearly did not know this, and was desperately asking for the foreign help promised to him. In response, Yahya Khan told him, 'White friends (Americans) will come from the south, and Yellow friends (Chinese) will come from the north.'[31]

It was, of course, an empty promise from a man who, by that time, was at a total loss on how to handle the situation.

□

Nair and Kao listened to the call between Niazi and Yahya Khan, and leaned back in their respective chairs.

'That went well,' Kao said mildly, and Nair grinned.

Both of them took a moment to savour the victory before Kao stood up. 'Let's call it a day, shall we?' he said, picking up his jacket, which had been resting on the back of his chair.

'Sure,' Nair said, but he remained seated. Kao knew the subtlest nuances of his friend's manner by then and looked at him, waiting for him to say what was on his mind.

'I heard that BBC report,' Nair said, looking pointedly at Kao.

'What report would that be?'

---

[31] Sukhwant Singh, *India's Wars Since Independence: The Liberation of Bangladesh*, (Vikas Publishing House, New Delhi, 1991), p. 219.

'The one that said 5,000 troops had been airdropped into Bangladesh.'

Radio stations as reputed as the British Broadcasting Company rarely got their information wrong. Mistakes are always bound to happen, particularly in a beat as hectic as war reporting, but the gross overstatement of 5,000 troops, while the actual number was only around 600, and that too on the part of the BBC, raised a few eyebrows.

The report was all the more significant because the All India Radio, as part of war strategy, was only allowed to report military activity two days after it had occurred, and that too after heavy censorship.

At their end, Radio Pakistan was so busy peddling lies against India, that it was known as Radio Jhootistan at R&AW. In this scenario, everyone, including Pakistan, depended on the BBC for whatever information they could get.

'Yes, curious, isn't it? For the BBC to be so far off the mark?'

'Was it?' Nair asked.

'Meaning?' Kao said.

'Are you, with a straight face, going to tell me that you played no part in planting this story to raise the collective blood pressure of the Pakistani Army and government?'

There was the slightest of smiles on Kao's face, which went away as quickly as it came.

'You know me, Nair,' Kao said. 'I can neither confirm nor deny that.'

Kao walked out of the room, lightly patting Nair on the shoulder before he left. Nair, who was well aware of his superior's secretive nature and fully understood his reasons, stood up with a smile and stated, almost as if to himself: 'All is fair in love and war.'

By 15 December 1971, the Mukti Bahini and allied forces had liberated Kustia to the west of Dhaka and Sylhet to its east. They had cleared out Comilla, Chittagong and Noakhali in the south.

The Indian Army had successfully penetrated Bangladesh and from all directions was closing in on Dhaka.

Chapter 15

The Last Council

WING COMMANDER BISHNOI HAD JUST RETURNED from a mission when Group Captain Wollen came running up to him. Captain Wollen explained to him that a very critical task had been assigned to them on an urgent basis from IAF headquarters.

R&AW had intercepted a message communicating that an important meeting was going to be conducted at the Circuit House in Dhaka, and the building needed to be bombed at 11.20 a.m.

Bishnoi was stunned. That gave him and his team less than half an hour to commence the attack, and it would take them at least twenty-one minutes to just get to Dhaka. Also, Bishnoi had no idea where the Circuit House was located.

In response, all he got was a tourist map of Dhaka with an 'x' marking their target. The building was in a densely populated area, and the slightest error on his team's part would lead to tremendous civilian casualties. But Bishnoi knew it was time to follow orders, no questions asked.

He set off with his team in four MiG-21s loaded with thirty-two explosive rockets. They were strapped in and had started the engines, preparing for take-off, when a flight commander came running up to Bishnoi and slapped a paper in his hand.

It was a small, square piece of paper, with only three lines written across it in neat, small handwriting:

> Target is Government House, repeat Government House and not Circuit House.
> Confirm understood.
> Best of luck and good shooting. Mall.[32]

Bishnoi and his team set off. They now had to make it to their target in fifteen minutes. The day was 14 December 1971, and Wing Commander Bishnoi would be the man who marked the beginning of the end of the war.

□

Earlier that morning at R&AW headquarters, Kao looked around at his team that had burnt the midnight oil for many months. The pressure was intense. Things

---

[32] B.K. Bishnoi, 'Thunder Over Dacca', excerpted from *Air Space*, January 1997 at https://www.bharat-rakshak.com/IAF/history/1971war/1271-thunder-over-dacca.html (10 January 2020).

were going according to plan, but they needed to seal
the deal before the UN called for a suspension of
hostilities.

India had put to use all the war strategies and
techniques at their disposal. For the past four days,
the IAF had been dropping pamphlets all over East
Pakistan, with particular focus on Dhaka. The flyers
urged the Pakistani Army to surrender and assured
them that they would be treated with the utmost
dignity and care if they did. Every day, several times
a day, hundreds of these pamphlets rained down on
military bases or locations with high concentration of
enemy troops in East Pakistan.

Manekshaw, too, had sent out a radio broadcast
directed at Pakistani soldiers, guaranteeing their
security if they surrendered to the Indian Army. He
promised that they would be evacuated from East
Pakistan, looked after in India, and sent home safely.
He also assured them that they would be guarded
against attack by hostile elements in East Pakistan.

The Mukti Bahini, which had now reached the
outskirts of Dhaka, was working with the ever-reliable
Tiger Siddiqui. They were garnering vast amounts of
local support every day. The Indian Army was also
about to reach Dhaka. The Pakistani soldiers were
now living in constant fear of an uprising from the
civilians.

However, Niazi, though demoralised by the losses his army had suffered, was determined to keep fighting. He had valiantly declared that Pakistan could keep up the fight for many months to come. Niazi was also well aware that, with each passing day, the possibility of a ceasefire induced by the UN increased.

At the UN, India's foreign minister Sardar Swaran Singh was having a tough time justifying India's actions in the ongoing war. Bhutto, who represented Pakistan with the backing of the US, was calling for an immediate ceasefire. Two proposals were tabled at the UN to this effect, one of them by China. The USSR, at India's request, had vetoed it both times. An enraged Bhutto had torn up the resolution in the UN assembly and walked out.

This bought India some time, but the Soviets had communicated to India that they would not veto the proposal again.

The danger was that if the UN ceasefire resolution came through before India had won the war, the painstaking mobilisation and long fight of the Mukti Bahini, the Mujib Bahini and the Indian armed forces for Bangladeshi independence would all be for nought, as Dhaka would still be under Pakistani control. After that, gaining freedom for East Bengal would be a painfully long-drawn process.

Added to the UN drama, R&AW was continuously intercepting Yahya Khan's reassuring messages to

Gen. Niazi that help was on its way from China and the US. While few in the agency and the government believed this to be true, India was nevertheless in a state of preparedness along the northern borders, in the unlikely event that the promised aid actually came.

All this meant that prolonging the war was simply not an option.

It was then that a breakthrough occurred. R&AW intercepted a message transmitted by radio in the early hours of 14 December, according to which the current cabinet of the East Pakistan government was to hold an emergency meeting at the Government House, the residence of East Pakistan governor, A.M. Malik.

Kao knew that this could be just what they needed. A strike on a vital target such as this one might just be the straw that would break the camel's back. The message was immediately relayed to IAF headquarters.

□

Wing Commander Bishnoi was airborne and headed for Dhaka. He and the other MiG-21s located the target building almost as soon as they arrived.

It was a beautiful and palatial old building with a large dome. There was a lush garden at its entrance. Bishnoi circled the target and confirmed its identity. Then he got back into the formation with his team. They were now perfectly poised for attack.

Meanwhile, on the ground, things weren't exactly idle.

Late the previous night, three Indian brigades had crossed the mighty Meghna River and were all set to attack Dhaka. They were armed with a 75/24 Howitzer gun that was carried across the Balu River, along with 168 shells. The plan was to fire it at different targets every half-hour until the enemy got the message. By the time Bishnoi's MiGs had approached Dhaka, the attack was well underway. In the meantime, Manekshaw kept up his calls, asking for surrender from Niazi.

As Bishnoi and his squadron circled the Government House, a crucial meeting was being held inside the building. It had been called by the governor to discuss a possible surrender and prevent additional loss of lives, loss of morale and loss of face.

There was an urgency in the tone of the meeting, owing to the situation, which clearly indicated that the leaders present were there to give their final seal of approval to the ceasefire and surrender.

By that time, everyone had realised that Yahya Khan did not have a handle on the situation; he was not interested in anything other than his beloved Scotch whiskey, parties and women. The corridors of power, or what was left of them, were still buzzing with reports of the previous night's party at Khan's newly constructed house in Peshawar. Even as the

Pakistani troops were struggling to keep up the last bits of their morale, Yahya Khan and the latest object of his affections, Mrs Shamim, along with other guests, were dancing drunk. Mrs Shamim, also known as the Black Pearl, was Pakistan's Ambassador to Austria at the time, and she was a Bengali. Maj. Gen. Ishtiaque, the military secretary, had had to physically restrain Yahya Khan when the latter insisted on dropping his beloved home, with no clothes on.

The meeting in the Government House had only just begun when, thanks to the deadly accuracy of Bishnoi and his squadron, four 57 mm rockets came piercing through the air. So precise was their aim that the rockets entered the building through its ventilators and brought the walls crashing down.

Even as debris rained all around them, Malik, who had managed to remain unhurt, crawled under a table. Scrambling, he dug a pen out from one pocket and a notepad from another. There, sitting under the half-broken wooden table, Malik first signed a proposal for a ceasefire and then wrote out his formal resignation from the post of governor of East Pakistan. Next, he then took off his shoes, found a bottle of water to wash his hands and feet, and knelt to offer namaz, knowing it might well be the last prayer of his life.

Minutes later, a second salvo of Indian rockets pierced the roof. Clinging to each other, Malik and the Cabinet members managed to escape with their lives. This was effectively the last meeting of an East Pakistan government. For all intents and purposes, the war was lost at that instant.

It was the IAF that had shot down three sabres in the Boyra bulge on 22 November 1971, initiating the 1971 Indo-Pak war. And it was the IAF's MiG-21 attack on the Government House in Dhaka on 14 December that ended the war. The circle was complete.

❑

The effects of the attack on Dhaka were immediate and definite.

The East Pakistan government ceased to exist on 14 December 1971. And with that, Niazi lost all hopes of outside help coming his way. Via radio, Yahya Khan sent a message to Gen. Niazi on 14 December 1971.

You have fought a heroic battle against overwhelming odds. The nation is proud of you and the world full of admiration. I have done all that is humanly possible to find an acceptable solution to the problem. You have now reached a stage where further resistance is no longer humanly possible, nor will it serve any useful purpose. It will only lead to a further loss of life and destruction. You should now take all necessary measures to stop the fighting and

preserve the lives of armed forces personnel,
all those from West Pakistan, and all loyal
elements. Meanwhile, I have moved the UN to
urge India to stop hostilities in East Pakistan
forthwith and to guarantee the safety of armed
forces and all other people who may be the
likely targets of miscreants.[33]

A depressed Niazi immediately contacted the office
of the American consul general, Herbert Spivack, to
arrange a ceasefire with the Indian government.

The same broadcast was also intercepted by R&AW's
radio interception division, where agents transcribed
it at a feverish pace and rushed it to the room where
Kao and Nair were monitoring live updates.

'Yahya Khan sent this on an open channel?' Nair
asked, surprised.

'Yes, sir,' the underling replied.

'Yahya Khan never ceases to amaze,' Nair said,
looking across the table at Kao.

At around 5 p.m., a diplomat in one of the consular
offices in Calcutta called a senior R&AW agent to
apprise him of Niazi's visit to Herbert Spivack, to
discuss what he said were proposals for ceasefire or
surrender. The R&AW agent then telephoned Herbert

---

[33] J.F.R. Jacob, *Surrender at Dacca: Birth of a Nation* (The University Press, Dhaka, 1997), p. 136.

Gordon, the US consul general at Calcutta, who denied any knowledge of the ceasefire. Next, the agent called Gen. Manekshaw and suggested he contact the American ambassador in Delhi. Manekshaw did so, but the ambassador stated that he did not know of any request to Spivack.

The question that plagued R&AW, the Indian forces and the PMO at this point was this: the ceasefire proposal was obviously meant for India, but if it had not reached any Indian office, where had it gone?

In fact, the proposal did not come to India until twenty-four hours had elapsed.

After Niazi had approached Spivack, he did send a message to their ambassador in Islamabad who then passed it on to Henry Kissinger, the US secretary of state. Kissinger, a friend of Yahya Khan, decided to give the Pakistan president one more day to reclaim the territory captured by Indian forces in western Pakistan before a ceasefire was announced. However, Yahya Khan had given up by then.

Gen. Manekshaw finally received the message on 15 December 1971. He immediately issued an assurance that Pakistani personnel would be extended every safety, provided they surrendered. The Pakistan Eastern Command was to contact the Indian Eastern Command at Fort William. The Pakistani commander-in-chief signalled Niazi to accept.

There was a sentiment in the country that West Pakistan should be shown their place before ending the war on the western front. But Prime Minister Indira Gandhi also declared a ceasefire on the western front, saying, 'If I don't do so today, I shall not be able to do so tomorrow.'[34]

The ceasefire came into effect from 5 p.m. on 15 December till 3 p.m. the next day.

The war had finally come to an end. There was a wave of celebrations all around the nation. Everywhere, people were hailing the victory of Indira Gandhi and the Indian armed forces. However, the general public was completely unaware of R&AW's existence and their contribution to the victory.

At R&AW headquarters, the small team celebrated their success privately. It was time for all of them to put their feet up finally.

A very tired Nair was putting on his jacket, looking forward to a restful slumber in his own bed for the first time in days, when there was a knock on his office door.

'Sorry, Nair,' Kao said, entering and locking the door behind him. 'We have one last thing to take care of.'

---

[34] Praveen Swami, *India, Pakistan and the Secret Jihad* (Routledge, New York, 2006), p. 121.

Chapter 16

Recoup

THE WAR WAS OVER.

India had taken approximately 93,000 prisoners of war (POWs), including Pakistani soldiers and their East Pakistani civilian supporters. It was the largest number of POWs taken into custody since World War II.

On 16 December 1971, Indira Gandhi stood in Parliament and declared, 'Dhaka is now the free capital of a free country. We hail the people of Bangladesh in their hour of triumph. All nations who value the human spirit will recognise it as a significant milestone in man's quest for liberty.'[35]

The entire world was talking about Pakistan's crushing defeat at the hands of India over the course of thirteen days. And the world's Intelligence community

---

[35] Gurmeet Kanwal, 'Bangladesh: India's Greatest Military Triumph', *Deccan Herald*, 16 December 2011, https://www.deccanherald.com/content/212050/liberation-bangladesh-indias-greatest-military.html (15 January 2020).

was abuzz with whispers about the new contender in the global espionage game—India's R&AW.

The fledgling agency, which until the Bangladesh liberation war had not been taken seriously by the big players like the CIA, had managed to orchestrate the freedom symphony of a whole country.

None of this, however, was Kao's concern at the moment. Locked away in the office, he and Nair had only one priority: getting Sheikh Mujibur Rahman out of Pakistan, alive.

Miles away, in Mianwali, Pakistan, Sheikh Mujibur Rahman sat calmly on the floor of his cell. It was the dawn of 15 December 1971. The first rays of the sun were just beginning to breach the darkness of the sky.

On 1 April that year, Rahman had been flown to Rawalpindi in West Pakistan, forcefully separated from his land and people by over a thousand miles of Indian territory. When he had been moved to the Mianwali prison, he was informed of the charges he had been accused of, for which he would be facing trial shortly.

Himself a lawyer, Rahman had known that he didn't have a snowball's chance in hell of being acquitted. Also, because he was a lawyer, he had realised that the best thing he could do under the circumstances was to delay the trial as much as possible. He asked to be defended by eminent lawyer A.K. Brohi, who took his time preparing the defence.

While on the other side of the border, Kao was running a race against time, on this side, Rahman was doing the opposite. Sheikh Mujibur Rahman used every tactic that he could to delay the court proceedings. He knew that Yahya Khan would not issue a death penalty before putting up the pretence of a fair trial. The Pakistan government would have to make it look like it had done everything in its power to protect his rights. Sheikh Mujibur Rahman's case hearing began on 11 August 1971.

By December 1971, Rahman had spent the last eight months alternating between prisons in Mianwali, Lyallpur and Sahiwal, all in the northern part of Pakistan's Punjab Province. His trial dragged on. And now he was on the verge of giving up hope. He had started preparing for his eventual death.

But war broke out before the verdict could be announced. And in just thirteen days, Pakistan had lost the battle. Bangladesh was a free nation—Rahman's dream. Along with the joy came the realisation that victory for Bangladesh meant immediate death for him. The angry people of West Pakistan would be baying for his blood now.

Kao was also aware of this fact. He had a solution in mind. The plan would have to be delicately executed. And it had to happen in London.

□

One afternoon, an attractive woman entered the VIP lounge at Heathrow International Airport in London. Several men turned, some almost involuntarily, to look at the undeniably beautiful lady as she walked past. She was only partly aware of the stares she was attracting, as she was looking for someone.

The woman walked at a steady pace through the lounge until she found the person she was looking for. He was busy working on a file in a corner of the lounge, away from the prying eyes of the crowd around him.

'Well, well,' she said as she slid into a chair beside the man. 'Isn't this a surprise?'

The man was taken aback. It was Zulfikar Ali Bhutto.

'Laila?' He looked at the woman next to him with mild surprise, sliding the file back into his briefcase.

They looked at each other silently for a moment. One did not need to be a genius to figure out that they had a shared history.

Among the thousands of people taken prisoner by the Indian forces when the war ended was one Muzaffar Hussain, former chief secretary of the East Pakistan government and the highest-ranking civil servant posted in Dhaka at the time of the war. During his imprisonment, Hussain was lodged, on Gandhi's orders, at the personal residence of D.P. Dhar, India's ambassador to the Soviet Union.

Laila Hussain was his wife. She was in London when the war broke out, and had since been stuck there. However, India had allowed her to communicate with her husband through diplomatic channels. The diplomat assigned to be the VIP courier was Sashanka S. Banerjee, who had just then been re-posted to East Pakistan after a successful stint there in 1961–65.

As the war neared its end, Kao realised that Pakistan would kill Rahman at the first available opportunity. The only thing that remained to be seen was how quickly Yahya Khan's whiskey-addled brain would think of it, and then the orders would be issued. Kao knew he had to move fast.

Even as he and Nair were trying to devise a plan to extract Rahman, the news came in that Bhutto had been appointed the chief martial law officer in Pakistan. Kao was about to file the information away in his mind when he stopped short. Two minutes later, even as Nair looked on impatiently, Kao smiled.

Like any good spy, Kao had files on all 'persons of interest' to India. Muzaffar Hussain was one of them, and by association, so was Laila. Kao smiled because he had suddenly recalled that Laila had been in a relationship with Bhutto before she married Hussain.

An audacious plan was set in motion involving Laila Hussain and Zulfikar Ali Bhutto. Sashanka Banerjee was to be the go-between.

Bhutto was on his way to Rawalpindi from Washington, and his flight had a stopover at Heathrow. This window of opportunity was quickly identified and grabbed with both hands. Sashanka Banerjee got in touch with Laila and persuaded her to meet with Bhutto in London.

As a pleasantly surprised Bhutto conversed with Laila in the VIP lounge at Heathrow, she made her move.

'Listen, Zulfikar, I ... I need a favour. For old times' sake?' Laila said earnestly.

'Sure,' a visibly melting Bhutto said. 'Anything.'

'It's my husband ... he's in Indian custody. I mean, he's being put up as a VIP guest, but he's still a prisoner of war. We haven't seen each other since this dreadful business began. You think ... you think you can help me to get him out of there, now that the war is over?'

Bhutto listened silently, but the gears of his brain were grinding hard. He waited for Laila to finish speaking. Then he leaned close and whispered in her ear. Three men who had been gazing at Laila with appreciation now burned with jealousy. Bhutto finished speaking, got up and walked away. So did Laila.

☐

'Laila, I know what you want. I can imagine you are [carrying a request] from Mrs Indira Gandhi. Do please pass a message to her, that after I take charge of office back home, I will shortly after that release Mujibur Rahman, allowing him to return home. What I want in return, I will let Mrs Indira Gandhi know through another channel. You may now go.'[36]

'That's all he said?' Nair asked.

'Banerjee says that's a direct quote from Laila,' Kao replied.

'Smart, that Bhutto,' Nair remarked.

Kao stood up and stretched his legs.

'One has to learn the tricks of the trade quickly, I believe. Hussain is the highest-ranking civil servant of his government that we have in our custody. At this point, Bhutto's priority has to be to secure all the POWs. Laila just provided a nudge in that direction. Bhutto knows he's holding the only bargaining chip he has against his POWs.'

❑

At Mianwali Prison, once the war broke out, Rahman had a fair idea of what was brewing around him, although he was unaware of the specifics. News of Pakistan losing the battle had already reached

---

[36] Sashanka S. Banerjee, 'The True Story of India's Decision to Release 93,000 Pakistani POWs After 1971 War', *The Wire*, 26 March 2017, https://thewire.in/history/the-untold-story-behind-indira-gandhis-decision-to-release-93000-pakistani-pows-after-the-bangladesh-war (19 November 2019).

the prison, and he knew that only a few possible outcomes could follow. The first result that Rahman anticipated was his own death at the hands of the Pakistani regime.

That belief was somewhat strengthened on the night of 15 December, when a small group of prisoners started digging what looked to him like a grave outside his cell. They maintained that it was just a trench to hold rainwater, but the 'trench' was dug right outside his cell and exactly the size needed to bury him in.

The other reason for his belief was his current location. Mianwali happened to be in Gen. Niazi's home district, which meant that many of the prisoners lodged with him would automatically consider him as their enemy. Rahman had no doubt that a plan was being drawn up to kill and bury him on the prison premises itself.

Even as he was contemplating his impending demise, he heard footsteps. They were hurried and light, only audible to someone who was listening for them, and kept getting closer. A shadow fell across his cell as a man stopped outside. Then, Rahman heard a key sliding into the lock and turning. The door to his cell swung open.

Rahman looked up calmly as the prison superintendent entered his cell.

'If you are going to kill me, janaab,' Rahman said, 'I'd like to offer namaaz first.'[37]

There was a moment's pause, and then the superintendent started pulling Rahman to his feet.

'There is no time for prayers,' the superintendent hissed and started pushing Rahman out of his cell. 'We must get out now. Before it is too late.'

That, Rahman had to admit, came as a surprise.

Rahman was led to a waiting jeep and then taken away, leaving the prison far behind. As the superintendent negotiated the turns on the road at a dangerously high speed, he told Rahman something that confirmed his suspicions. The prisoners at Mianwali had indeed been plotting to kill him. They had been told that Niazi had been killed in the war—the war that Rahman had started. They had readily agreed to bludgeon Rahman to death with their bare hands and bury him in the prison compound.

At considerable personal risk, the prison superintendent drove Sheikh Mujibur Rahman to his own house, where both Rahman and the officer spent two nerve-wracking days, expecting a raid by men armed to the teeth any minute. The only thing they had going for them was that there was a lot of confusion in the official circles as the war was nearing

[37] Sydney H. Schanberg, 'He Tells Full Story of Arrest and Detention', *The New York Times*, 18 January 1972.

its end, which meant that Rahman's disappearance from his Mianwali prison cell might not be noticed at the higher echelons immediately.

□

It was 16 December 1971. The war was over, Rahman had escaped prison, and another event was unfolding in Bangladesh.

Early that morning, Maj. Gen. J.F.R. Jacob had landed in Dhaka with a staff officer. He was carrying the Instrument of Surrender with him.

Jacob was chief of staff of the Indian Army's Eastern Command. Accompanied by his aide, he reached Niazi's office, where senior Pakistani Army, Navy and Air Force officers had assembled. Maj. Gen. Gandharva Singh Nagra, commander of the two mountain brigades of the Indian Army, was present as well.

Nagra later told Jacob that Niazi broke down in front of him. 'He said something about being let down by *pindi mein baithe haramzaade* (the bastards sitting in Rawalpindi).'[38]

Jacob handed over the Instrument of Surrender for Niazi to sign. Gen. Rao Farman Ali of the Pakistani

---

[38] Inam Ahmad and Shakhawat Liton, 'Sun Rose From Ruins', *The Daily Star*, 16 December 2015 https://www.thedailystar.net/frontpage/nagras-lightening-advance-187612 (16 January 2020).

6666

Army read out the terms of the surrender. As expected, Niazi was not in the mood to go down without a fight. He refused, telling Jacob that he wasn't going to surrender. It was only a ceasefire, he insisted.

That was when Jacob decided on a rather dangerous gamble.

'I have offered you terms that are in line with the Geneva Convention, sir,' Jacob said calmly but firmly. 'I give you thirty minutes to consider the proposal. If, after that, you choose to stick to your stand, I will order the resumption of hostilities.'[39]

Jacob returned to Niazi precisely in half an hour.

'General,' Jacob asked, laying down the document of surrender on Niazi's table again. 'Do you accept this document?'

Jacob repeated his question two more times, but Niazi stayed silent. Jacob picked it up.

'I take it as accepted,' he said. 'Now you will surrender publicly in front of the people of Dhaka.'[40]

Niazi looked up for the first time. There were tears in his eyes. The other top-ranking officials of the Pakistani Army were silent too, but their eyes held unbridled hatred.

---

[39] J.F.R Jacob, *An Odyssey in War and Peace* (Roli Books, New Delhi, 2011), p. 180.

[40] J.F.R. Jacob, *Surrender at Dacca: Birth of a Nation* (The University Press, Dhaka, 1997), p. 143.

Jacob suddenly felt very alone in an extremely hostile environment. He stepped out of the room and lit his pipe.

◻

The public place chosen for the signing of the Instrument of Surrender was the racecourse at Dhaka.

At the appointed time, Tiger Siddiqui, the guerrilla hero of the war, came roaring up the tarmac with a truck full of Mukti Bahini soldiers.

'Guns ready,' Jacob snapped at the paratroopers accompanying him. They raised their guns, faces tense.

Jacob walked over to Siddiqui, who was storming towards him anyway, and they met midway.

'Where's Niazi?' Siddiqui growled.

'Listen to me, Siddiqui,' Jacob said. 'No one has any doubts about the part you have played in the war and the entire country, including the prime minister, has nothing but praise for you. But if you harm a single hair on Niazi's head, the surrender, which goes down today, will be called off and we'll be at war again.'

'I don't care,' Siddiqui said through gritted teeth.

'You do,' Jacob said. 'We all do. Nobody wants any more bloodshed, on either side. And even if you don't, my boys will not hesitate to shoot you if you stand in my path any longer. I'm going back to tell them that, and by the time I turn around, you better be out of my way.'

Jacob walked back to his group, issued the instructions to his paratroopers, and turned around. They walked calmly past Siddiqui, who continued to burn a hole into Jacob's back with his murderous gaze till he was out of sight.

The Instrument of Surrender was signed by Lt. Gen. A.A.K. Niazi of the Pakistan Army at Ramna Race Course in Dhaka on 16 December 1971. He surrendered to Lt. Gen. Jagjit Singh Aurora, joint commander of the Bangladesh–India Allied Forces at 4.31 p.m., Indian Standard Time.

The Bangladeshis gathered to witness this historic moment at the racecourse erupted in loud cheers. The joy on their faces was unbridled.

◻

Still in his office at R&AW headquarters on Lodhi Road, Kao had only one thing on his mind—where exactly was Sheikh Mujibur Rahman, and would Bhutto keep his end of the bargain?

Rahman spent nine days in the house of the police superintendent, from 15 December to 25 December 1971. He was surviving on a limited ration of food and water, which the superintendent had managed to provide him on the day he had taken him there. Bringing supplies every day was not an option as there was every possibility that the superintendent was being watched.

On the tenth day, the superintendent came bearing news. A squad of soldiers from the Pakistan Army had visited him that morning and asked about Rahman's whereabouts.

'Times have changed,' the soldier had told the superintendent. 'Janaab, Bhutto has assumed power. And he has no interest in killing Rahman. I'm not saying you know where Rahman is. I'm just saying this is something Rahman should be aware of.'

Rahman listened to the superintendent's words and thought hard.

'Take me to Bhutto,' he said finally.

The superintendent arranged a meeting between the soldiers and Rahman. That same evening, Rahman was flown to Rawalpindi and taken to the president's guest house. He and the superintendent had hugged each other for a long moment before they parted ways. Both of them had tears in their eyes.

In Delhi, Kao was informed that Sheikh Mujibur Rahman had surfaced in Rawalpindi and that a meeting was to take place between Bhutto and Rahman.

On 19 December 1971, Bhutto took over the reins of the country from the discredited generals. This was the same Bhutto who, as the leader of the majority party in West Pakistan, had collaborated with the armed forces and ordered the crackdown in East Pakistan.

When Yahya Khan had met Bhutto for the last time, Khan was bitter and expressed his regret at the fact that he had not been able to finish off 'this one piece of work'.

Now Bhutto was standing face to face with Yahya Khan's 'piece of work', Sheikh Mujibur Rahman.

'I am the president and also the chief martial law administrator,' Bhutto said, making himself comfortable on a sofa chair in the room. 'A wonderful situation, wouldn't you say?'[41]

Rahman said nothing but moved from his position and sat on the bed in front of Bhutto's chair. He was thinking of the old adage: politics and war make strange bedfellows.

A year ago, Rahman would not have wanted to be in the same room with Bhutto. And yet, Bhutto was the one hope that Rahman had that day of returning alive to his people. He had read in the newspapers that India held thousands of Pakistani POWs, and he suspected that he was going to be Bhutto's bargaining chip in the exchange.

After the war, Yahya Khan had offered to sign pre-dated papers ordering Rahman's execution so that Bhutto could fulfil his wish. Personally, Bhutto did not care if Rahman lived or died, but for political reasons,

---

[41] Sydney H. Schanberg, 'He Tells Full Story of Arrest and Detention', *The New York Times*, 18 January 1972.

he had to refuse. He knew that if Bangabandhu was executed, it would lead to the deaths of nearly 100,000 Pakistani soldiers who had surrendered to the Indian forces, and that he, Bhutto, would end up taking the blame. He was certainly not taking that risk for the sake of a petty enmity that a drunk and defeated man refused to let go of.

'Am I a prisoner or am I free?' was all that Rahman asked Bhutto.

'You're free,' Bhutto said as he rose from his seat and started walking away. 'But it will be some days before you can go home.'[42]

□

Meanwhile, things were developing fast on the international front.

While Rahman was lodged in the president's guest house, demanding that Bhutto release him every time the latter came to visit him, the newly formed country of Bangladesh was seeking diplomatic recognition from countries around the world. Only a few countries had recognised Bangladesh as an independent nation when Pakistan surrendered to India.

Bangladesh also sought admission to the UN, but the proposal was vetoed by China at the time, as Pakistan

---

[42] Sydney H. Schanberg, 'He Tells Full Story of Arrest and Detention', *The New York Times*, 18 January 1972.

was its ally. The US, also an ally of Pakistan, was the last country to accord recognition to Bangladesh.

In India, meanwhile, Gandhi was constantly negotiating and finalising the terms of the exchange with Bhutto.

At the time of the ceasefire, Pakistan had not achieved any of the objectives that were chalked out when the war began. It had captured no large tracts of Indian territory that could be used as bargaining chips for East Pakistan. Not only had Pakistan suffered a massive loss of men and material in the war, but nearly a lakh of its men were now POWs in India.

India was dealing with her own problems, too. She had borne the cost of the war, and now she had to take on the financial burden of nearly 10 million refugees who had crossed over to India from East Pakistan. The Pakistani POWs only added to this burden.

◻

Ever since Bhutto had taken over from Yahya Khan, he had tried his best to convince Rahman to maintain a political alliance between West Pakistan and Bangladesh. But Rahman did not relent. Finally, Bhutto made his decision. It was time for Rahman to go home.

The day was 10 January 1971. The place was Dhaka. The atmosphere, in a word, could be described as festive, and for good reason.

Sheikh Mujibur Rahman had been put on an exclusive jet from Rawalpindi by Bhutto. Rahman first travelled to London, where he addressed the international press. Then he was taken to a hospital for a check-up. From London, he flew to Delhi where Indira Gandhi received him. In Delhi, he attended a celebration with top-ranking officials of the Indian government. He also met up with Kao, Nair, his old friend P.N. Banerjee, and many others who had championed his cause from India.

From Delhi, Rahman took a flight to Dhaka.

Thousands of people lined the street that their beloved Bangabandhu was to take. A jeep appeared in the distance. Rahman was standing in the back of the open jeep, waving to his people with tears in his eyes. The people pressed closer. The emotion in the air was almost tangible. Hundreds of men, women and children were crying openly.

'*Joy Bangla!*' Rahman said.

'*JOY BANGLA!*' the crowd roared back.

Some men in the crowd raised a slogan of their own.

'*Joy Bangabandhu!*'

The crowd roared again.

'*JOY BANGABANDHU!*'

In India, this spectacle was watched silently by two men—R.N. Kao and K. Sankaran Nair. They were the sculptors of modern Bangladesh, the men who had managed to bring the crown prince, Sheikh Mujibur Rahman, safely back to his homeland to assume his rightful throne.

Epilogue

THE THIRTEEN-DAY WAR WAS OVER, THE INSTRUMENT of Surrender had been signed, and Sheikh Mujibur Rahman was back home, alive and well, and leading his new country.

The R&AW office at Lodhi Road had fallen back into the daily rhythm it had established since 21 September 1968.

Kao addressed his core team. 'Intelligence is a complex game. The knower's powers lie in knowing, not in acting; that job is reserved for heroes.'

For Kao and his team, there would be no victory parades, no public celebrations and no awards conferred while people applauded. Very few knew who had held the reins of the 'special assignment'. The credit would never be acknowledged in public, no matter the enormousness of the task or the magnitude of its impact. But those in the know in the Indian armed forces and in the journalist fraternity bestowed accolades upon R&AW in private. They praised the meticulous planning and orchestration of the unconventional guerrilla resistance in East Pakistan.

By and large though, their role in the liberation war remained undisclosed. Many in R&AW did not even know that the organisation was directly involved in the war. Not many in the government, or even in their own families, would ever know how tirelessly they had worked to bring the new nation into existence. R&AW had ensured that the first significant mission assigned to them after their conceptualisation in 1968 had turned out to be a stunning success.

It was this success in the 1971 war that would catapult the organisation into the annals of spy history. Kao knew that this was a story that would be remembered by generations to come. What more is there to life than to have ventured into a stimulating adventure of such an epic scale, a revolutionary war for independence that led to the birth of a new country.

But these were just the first steps for the still-young agency, and Kao knew that the next steps were critical.

❑

The foundations of R&AW were solid. Kao had extremely trustworthy deputies in K. Sankaran Nair, M.B.K. Nair and P.N. Banerjee, among others.

As a team led by Kao, they had done a phenomenal job—not only providing Intelligence to safeguard India at a critical phase in the long conflict with her neighbour Pakistan, but also helping to lay the foundations of freedom for the brand-new state of Bangladesh.

In the process, Kao's men had tapped into their spy networks, established personal relationships with key players, and also set up state-of-the-art monitoring and Intelligence systems.

Kao knew that the victory of the war belonged to his men as much as to the defence forces of the country. But he was also aware, that despite all the praise being showered on them, the organisation had its shortcomings. And he resolved to start the next innings of R&AW by addressing them.

Led by Kao, a specialised team conducted an extensive study of all events before and during the war. They identified two glaring deficiencies: one, there had been inefficiency in collecting maritime Intelligence in the Indian Ocean; and two, they hadn't yet established a channel of Intelligence for the US and its activities against India.

While no one denied the fact that 1971 had been R&AW's finest hour yet, these two failings would have to be addressed—and fast.

On the other hand, post-war, Indira Gandhi had other political issues which needed immediate attention.

Gandhi had come under heavy criticism for not including the return of Pakistan-Occupied Kashmir

(POK) as one of the demands after the war. Many saw India's victory as an opportunity to sort out the Kashmir issue once and for all. But Gandhi made it clear that the political objective of the war did not extend beyond the scope of the liberation of Bangladesh.

Pakistan was already naming India as a co-conspirator with Bangladesh in their freedom struggle, and talking about the Kashmir issue at this juncture would only confirm the Pakistani accusation that India had been motivated by an imperialist agenda. India's support of Bangladesh in the Muktijuddho had not been a pre-planned conspiratorial strategy. It was a politico-strategic response to the continuous threats which Pakistan had been posing to the unity and integrity of India since 1947. Bringing the Kashmir issue to the negotiating table with Pakistan would simply have diluted India's efforts to free Bangladesh.

□

On 2 August 1972, the two countries signed the Simla Agreement, under which India agreed to release all the 93,000 Pakistani POWs its army had taken during the war.

The war of 1971 was the greatest crisis that Pakistan had faced since its formation in 1947. The dismembered Pakistan was left with only the four provinces of West

Pakistan: Punjab, Sindh, the North-western Frontier Province, and Baluchistan. They had lost a province of 70 million people which constituted 56 per cent of their original population, and over 1,47,670 square kilometres of territory.

Yahya Khan was presumed to be the primary cause of this disaster. He had 'failed to inspire respect and confidence in the mind of his subordinates'.[43] Disillusionment, uncertainty and pessimism had prevailed.

On 20 December 1971, Yahya Khan had handed over the presidency to Bhutto. And slowly, Pakistan started recuperating under the leadership of Zulfikar Ali Bhutto. Bhutto immediately took steps to revitalise the economy, industry and agriculture. He drew up a new constitution and re-established civilian authority over the armed forces in the political setup. Sheikh Mujibur Rahman had been released and returned safely to Bangladesh, while Yahya Khan had been confined to 'house arrest'. During his confinement, Yahya Khan was paralysed by a stroke.

□

On 12 January 1972, the new government of Bangladesh was formed. Sheikh Mujibur Rahman

---

[43] 'Tragic Events of 1971: Hamoodur Rahman Commission Report Excerpts', *India Today*, reproduced in *The Daily Star*.

stepped down from the role of 'president' to be re-elected as Bangladesh's prime minister.

Bangabandhu could not sustain the joy that the country had felt upon achieving its liberation. The world's newest nation was also one of its poorest. In Bangladesh, Rahman had inherited a child in need of intensive care. It was a struggling state with no police force, no navy, no civil aviation, and no infrastructure for a competent civil government. They had 75 million mouths to feed, and no source of wealth. The country had to start from nothing.

Rahman found temporary monetary help in the form of loans from the World Bank and some East European communist countries. He had to work hard at rebuilding the damaged jute industry, which had been the region's primary source of income in 1969–70. Bangladesh also struggled to revive its ruined tea gardens. They were relying on foreign aid and food relief, while building the transportation system from the ground up.

□

Meanwhile, India and Pakistan were coming to terms with the aftermath of the war. Both countries needed to recover financially and were in favour of a diplomatic settlement after the conflict. The espionage teams of both countries had declared a truce too, but internally, the teams continued to engage in a game of one-upmanship.

Pakistan's ISI was the country's conventional intelligence agency which reported to its army chief. Despite their seniority—ISI was created in 1948—they had had a hard time keeping up with R&AW's path-breaking work during the 1971 war. Post-war, Bhutto set up a war enquiry commission to look into the workings of Pakistani Intelligence, and analyse the failures of the ISI as well as the army during the conflict.

In India, Kao and his team of boys had been nicknamed 'Kaoboys'. The team was proud of its leader and mentor. But Kao, in his humility, had only smiled when he had first heard the name. His aim had been very straightforward; he had wanted to raise a team which worked in perfect synchrony towards their common goal—ensuring the security and integrity of India. He had been pleased to see the outcome of their first mission, and was now confident that his 'boys' were ready for what he had in mind for them next.

As Kao's confidence and Gandhi's trust in him grew, R&AW started setting up several offices inside and outside the country. Locations such as Madras, Bombay, Calcutta, Lucknow, Patna, Cochin and Bangalore were selected with a view to looking for possible sources among those visiting India from abroad.

◻

Barely two years after the war, in 1974, R&AW pulled off another feat—this time, within the country's borders. It would be the first time that R&AW was working in-house in complete secrecy.

The world at large knows of it as Pokhran-I.

On 18 May 1974, India conducted its first successful test of a nuclear bomb at the Pokhran testing range in Rajasthan. The operation was called 'Smiling Buddha', and the name carries its legends with it.

Some say that it was because the day the nuclear test was performed happened to be Buddha Jayanti. Others say that it was named after the Buddha, who devoted his life to preaching peace and non-violence, and the Pokhran mission was aimed at establishing peace around the world. With Smiling Buddha, India became the world's sixth nuclear power, after the US, Soviet Union, Britain, France and China.

Besides the team at Pokhran, the only Indians who knew of the test in advance were Indira Gandhi and two of her close advisers, Dhar and Haksar. Gandhi would forever marvel at the fact that there was no written record or report of the operation. Everything was oral, and on a strict need-to-know basis. Years later, almost the entire operation was documented based on the recollections of the R&AW team involved.

□

Eventually, the legend of the 'Kaoboys' spread far and wide.

George W. Bush, when he held office as the director of the CIA from November 1975 to January 1977, became a close friend of Kao's. While the relationship between the CIA and the R&AW tended to blow hot and cold, their friendship remained strong. Bush had heard from the CIA station chief in New Delhi that Kao and his officers were fondly called the Kaoboys of R&AW. When Kao paid a visit to the CIA headquarters in Washington, D.C., Bush gifted him a small bronze statue of a cowboy.

Kao kept the statue on the table in his office. Later, he had a giant replica of this statue made by Sadiq, a sculptor from Calcutta. Sadiq made the face of the cowboy resemble Kao. It was Kao's gift to his team at R&AW.

Despite the accolades Kao received throughout this career, his most significant achievement—the war of 1971—turned out, ironically, to be the very reason his capabilities were challenged.

On 15 August 1975, Bangladesh lost its hero, Sheikh Mujibur Rahman. Rahman was assassinated as part of a coup d'etat, in a bloodbath which also claimed many members of his family.

An impression has persisted even in R&AW that, after 1971, it lost touch with Bangladesh and was no longer well-informed about the new neighbour it had helped create. Over the years since then, R&AW's judgements about Pakistan had proved correct more often than its estimates about Bangladesh.

By 1973, although the Awami League had won 282 seats out of 289 in the elections, corruption and mismanagement were turning popular sentiment away from Mujib. In these chaotic conditions, R&AW had failed to diversify contacts in Bangladesh. There was rising hostility among its security forces and Intelligence community towards India and R&AW. Suspicion and resentment in the non-Awami League circles grew, a reaction to what was perceived as Indian favouritism towards certain sections of the political spectrum. This accelerated the decline of R&AW's performance in Bangladesh.

Kao, however, had continued inconspicuously to track events and developments in the neighbouring country. He was aware of the growing unpopularity of Sheikh Mujibur Rahman, particularly amongst the Bangladeshi armed forces. He began to hear whispers of plots being hatched against Rahman.

R&AW had received Intel of an alleged meeting between Maj. Rashid, Maj. Farooq and

Lt. Col. Usmani at Ziaur Rahman's residence four months before the assassination of the prime minister. This was the same Ziaur Rahman who had read out the first declaration of Bangladesh's independence on 27 March 1971 from the Kalurghat radio station in Chittagong.

The outcome of the meeting, among other things, had been the decision to stage a coup. During the three-hour session, one of the participants had doodled on a scrap of paper, which had then been carelessly thrown into a wastebasket. The piece of paper had been retrieved from the rubbish pile by a clerk and passed on to a R&AW operative. The information had eventually reached New Delhi.

Breaking all previous protocol, Kao had flown into Dhaka undercover, posing as a paan exporter and betel nut seller. He was then driven to a pre-arranged rendezvous point.

Mujib had found the entire exercise highly dramatic and failed to understand why Kao could not have paid him an official visit.

The Kao–Mujib meeting lasted one hour. Kao was unable to convince Rahman that a coup was brewing and that his life was in danger. This, despite his giving Mujib the names of those suspected to have been involved.

Four months later, the prime minister of Bangladesh

perished, along with several members of his family and personal staff, in a bloody mass murder.

'It was an army manoeuvre,' Kao told Gandhi after the massacre. 'The Bengal Lancers and the Bangla Desh Armoured Corps moved out of the cantonment to the capital's half-built airport. A few hours later, forty members of the household, along with Sheikh Mujib himself, were found dead. Nair's sources tell him that the killings took all of three minutes.'

Across the desk in her office, Gandhi listened stonily. There was a minute of silence before she spoke. 'What now?'

'The usual, I presume. They'll blame me. Then they'll blame you. Maybe both will happen together. The rumour mills are already gathering steam.'

'We did try, didn't we?'

'You know we did, madam,' Kao said.

She was the only person, apart from Nair, who knew of his visit to Bangladesh.

Kao and Gandhi were thinking the same thing: There will be successes, and there will be failures. There will be detractors, and there will be allies. If there was one thing that would remain constant, it was the country. And the country needed them to keep working.

Years later, a junior officer at R&AW asked Kao, 'How could R&AW not have known about the assassination and the coup?'

To which he replied, 'All I can say is, we were not surprised by the turn of events.'[44]

□

But tragedy and death did not end with Sheikh Mujibur Rahman. Rahman's death was followed by a setback of a more personal nature to Kao and R&AW.

They lost one of their Kaoboys, P.N. Banerjee, under mysterious circumstances.

Banerjee was a key agent at R&AW, one on whom Kao had relied heavily during the 1971 war. He was a close confidant of Rahman as well, and had been a vital courier and peacebuilder between India and Bangladesh.

Banerjee had pulled off another grand operation in 1971. He had come to know that an officer of the Awami League, Khondaker Mostaq, had been working for the Americans during the war. Mostaq, operating out of the Awami League's temporary headquarters in Mujib Nagar in Calcutta, had been passing on information to the CIA. Instead of confronting him, Banerjee had played an intelligent double game. He decided to use Mostaq to mislead the Americans about Indian plans. Under the pretext of tackling Naxalites, the Indian Army had deployed for a final push into East Pakistan.

---

[44] Interview with Vappala Balachandran, retd special secretary, 12 December 2019.

However, Banerjee sold Mostaq the story that India was in no condition to go for military intervention because it had rebellions in the Northeast and Naxalite activity in West Bengal to handle. The Americans found out much later why their information about India had been so wrong.

Banerjee died suddenly and mysteriously in Dhaka in 1974. Many in India and R&AW believe that Banerjee's mysterious death was not the cardiac arrest it was made out to be.

□

Kao realised that although the war was won and a new nation had been formed, death was the ultimate reality and it would prevail. Before the end of the decade, all the key leaders who were heavily invested in the 1971 war would be dead.

In Pakistan, a military coup staged by Zia-ul-Haq overthrew Zulfikar Ali Bhutto from his post as prime minister in 1977. He was banned from active politics, and multiple charges were levied against him, including that of murder. Bhutto was imprisoned and hanged to death in 1979.

An ailing Yahya Khan was still under house arrest in 1979. He was released in 1980, but by then he was weak from years of alcohol abuse and ill health. He died in Rawalpindi in 1980.

Kao maintained a relative distance from all that was happening and continued to work loyally for the country.

India herself went through tumultuous times in 1975. Indira Gandhi declared a state of Emergency in India, leading to a political uprising that swept the nation.

After the debacle of the Emergency, Indira Gandhi was voted out of power in 1977, and Morarji Desai succeeded her. Kao tried his best to continue his espionage journey with Desai, but unfortunately, he couldn't win his trust.

Kao quit as head of R&AW in 1977 due to alleged differences with Desai. And his trusted aide Sankaran Nair took over as the new R&AW chief.

In 1980, Indira Gandhi came back to power for the third time. Kao returned as security advisor to both Indira Gandhi and Rajiv Gandhi in the same year.

Kao continued to help the R&AW, and his boys took up essential tasks for the country. He was the architect of the National Security Guard, created in the 1980s to counter insurgency in Punjab.

Indira Gandhi was assassinated by her Sikh bodyguards in 1984 in a visceral response to Operation Blue Star. Her death devastated Kao. His long-standing association with Indira Gandhi had developed into a close personal bond.

Not long after, Kao retired and lived a peaceful life thereafter, spending time with family at his home. The life of a spy is lived in the shadows, and Kao lived by that tenet even after his retirement. However, he was always available for consultation on matters related to the nation's security.

The Oxford Dictionary defines a hero as 'a person who is admired for their courage, outstanding achievements and noble qualities'. There can be no doubt that Rameshwar Nath Kao, in the truest sense of the word, was a hero.

Bibliography

Abdul Mannan, 'The Big Bird and Narratives of a General', *Daily Sun*, 26 March 2018, https://www.daily-sun.com/printversion/details/297831/2018/03/26/The-Big-Bird-and-Narratives-of-a-General

Aditi De, 'Indira Gandhi: A Study in Leadership in India's Democracy', University of Calcutta, Research Paper, Shodhganga, https://shodhganga.inflibnet.ac.in/handle/10603/164817

Ahmad Faruqui, 'The Betrayal of East Pakistan', *Media Monitors*, 27 June 2001, https://www.mediamonitors.net/the-betrayal-of-east-pakistan/

Ahsaan Akram, 'Hijacking Ganga and the Case of Hashim Qureshi', *Oracle Opinions*, 11 December 2018, https://oracleopinions.com/2018/12/11/hijacking-ganga-and-the-case-of-hashim-qureshi/

Aminur Rahman, 'Operation Jackpot', *Defence Forum India*, 3 September 2012, https://defenceforumindia.com/operation-jackpot-1-538, https://defenceforumindia.com/operation-jackpot-2-571

Anshul Gandhi, 'Operation HAT: How CIA Lost a Nuclear Device in India While Spying on China and Almost Polluted Ganga', 21 November 2017, https://www.mensxp.com/special-features/longform/39854-operation-hat-how-cia-lost-a-nuclear-device-in-india-while-spying-on-china-and-almost-polluted-ganga.html

Antara Dutta, *Refugees and Borders in South Asia: The Great Exodus of 1971* (Routledge, New York, 2012).

Anthony Mascarenhas, 'Genocide', *The Daily Star*, 16 December 2017, https://www.thedailystar.net/supplements/victory-day-special-2017/genocide-1505440

Anwar Hussain, 'Operation Jackpot Retold: "It was like a Suicide Mission"', *Dhaka Tribune*, 15 December 2016, https://www.dhakatribune.com/bangladesh/2016/12/15/operation-jackpot

Arjimand Hussain Talib, 'Hijack That Changed History', *Greater Kashmir*, 14 March 2015, https://www.greaterkashmir.com/news/gk-magazine/hijack-that-changed-history/

Arundhati Roy, 'The Working of the Indo-Soviet Treaty (1971–1986)', Jawaharlal Nehru University, Research Paper, Shodhganga, https://shodhganga.inflibnet.ac.in/handle/10603/14233

Asoka Raina, *Inside R&AW* (Vikas Publishing House, New Delhi, 1982).

AVM (Retd.) B.K. Bishnoi, 'Thunder over Dacca 1971', excerpted from *Air Space*, January 1997, http://www.bharat-rakshak.com/IAF/History/1971War/Dacca.html (accessed 10 January 2020).

AVM Arjun Subramaniam (Retd.), 'Even before 1971 War Started with Pakistan, India Had Won the Battle', *The Print*, 22 November 2018, https://theprint.in/opinion/even-before-1971-war-started-with-pakistan-india-had-won-the-battle/152975/

Azizur Rahman Anik, 'March 7: The Speech That Gave Birth to Bangladesh', *The Business Standard*, 8 March 2020, https://tbsnews.net/thoughts/march-7-speech-gave-birth-bangladesh-53305

B. Raman, 'Those Nuclear Ice Spies', *Outlook India*, 28 April 2003, https://www.outlookindia.com/magazine/story/those-nuclear-ice-spies/219931

B. Raman, *The Kaoboys of R&AW: Down Memory Lane* (Lancer Publishers, New Delhi, 2007).

B.N. Sharga, 'The Czar of India's Counter Intelligence', 15 December 2019, https://ikashmir.net/rnkao/czar.html

Bangladesh Genocide Archive, http://www.genocidebangladesh.org/timeline/

Batabyal Guru Saday, 'Politico-military Strategy of Bangladesh Liberation War 1971,' Visva Bharti University, Research Paper, Shodhganga, https://shodhganga.inflibnet.ac.in/handle/10603/22 1627

Blog, *Return of Bangabandhu*, 9 October 2017, http://www.londoni.co/index.php/64-history-of-bangladesh/biography/

sheikh-mujibur-rahman-bangabandhu/324-sheikh-mujibur-rahman-bangabandhu-return-of-bangabandhu-re-building-bangladesh-biography-of-muslim-and-bengali

Chandrashekhar Bhattacharya, 'Ramji Kao: Seven Things You Must Know about the Legendary Spymaster, 11 May 2018, http://delhidefencereview.com/2018/05/11/ramji-kao-seven-things-you-must-know-about-the-legendary-spymaster/

Colonel Abhay Patwardhan (Retd), 'Indo Pak War of 1971: A Glorious Chapter in India's History', NewsBharati, 17 December 2017, https://www.newsbharati.com/Encyc/2017/12/17/1971-War-A-glorious-chapter-in-India-s-history.html

Commodore Abdul Wahed Chowdhury, 'Naval Commandos in Operation Jackpot', *The Daily Star*, 26 March 2015, https://www.thedailystar.net/supplements/independence-day-special-2015/submariners-heroism-and-the-first-military-response-france

David Ludden, 'The Politics of Independence of Bangladesh', *Economic & Political Weekly*, Vol. 46, No. 35 (27 August 2011), p. 79 https://www.epw.in/journal/2011/35/perspectives/politics-independence-bangladesh.html

Dewan Shamsul Arefin, *Maulana Bhashani* (Xlibris US, 2018).

Directorate General of Infantry, *Field Marshall KM Kariappa Memorial Lectures, 1995-2000* (Lancer Publishers: New Delhi, 2001), p. 29.

Dishi Bora, 'Operation Smiling Buddha: India's First Successful Nuclear Bomb Test', *The Fact Research*, 5 February 2019, https://www.thefactresearch.com/operation-smiling-buddha/

Economic Times, 'When Yahya Khan Gave Inkling of His Intention to Attack India', *Economic Times*, 15 January 2012, https://economictimes.indiatimes.com/articleshow/11497848.cms?from=mdr&utm_source=contentofinterest&utm_medium=text&utm_campaign=cppst

Gary J. Bass, *The Blood Telegram: Nixon, Kissinger and a Forgotten Genocide* (Alfred A. Knopf, New York, 2013).

Gulshan Luthra, '1971 War: BBC Report, An Error or a Plant?'

India Strategic, December 2011, https://www.indiastrategic.in/topstories1314_1971_war_BBC_report.htm

Gurmeet Kanwal, 'Bangladesh: India's Greatest Military Triumph', *Deccan Herald*, 16 December, 2011, https://www.deccanherald.com/content/212050/liberation-bangladesh-indias-greatest-military.html

Hassan Abbas, *Pakistan's Drift into Extremism: Allah, then Army, and America's War Terror* (Routledge, 2004).

Howard Whitten, 'Fight for Life as Aid Reaches Stricken Isles', *The Guardian*, 18 November 1970, https://www.theguardian.com/world/2014/nov/18/bhola-cyclone-manpura-east-pakistan-bangladesh-1970

http://www.docstrangelove.com/uploads/1971/foreign/19710527_guardian_letter_east_bengal_atrocities.pdf

http://www.genocidebangladesh.org/timeline/

https://bdcgtoronto.ca/index.php/father-of-the-nation/

https://mujib100.gov.bd/pages/mujib/speeches.html

https://www.nytimes.com/1972/02/07/archives/mrs-gandhi-opens-talks-with-mujib-defense-and-economic-pact.html

https://www.thedailystar.net/supplements/history-written-blood-187984

https://www.youtube.com/watch?v=mqeU7dTAQPM

https://www.youtube.com/watch?v=SxVJhbFir6A

Inam Ahmed and Shakhawat Liton, 'Sun Rose from Ruins', *The Daily Star*, 16 December 2015, https://www.thedailystar.net/frontpage/nagras-lightening-advance-187612 (accessed 16 January 2020).

Inam Ahmed and Shakhawat Liton, 'Pakistan Lying, Still: Genocide Plot Conceived at Duck Shooting Trip', *The Daily Star*, 4 December 2015, https://www.thedailystar.net/frontpage/genocide-finalised-duck-shooting-trip-182089

India Today, 'When a Kashmiri Teen Hijacked a Plane with a Toy Pistol', *India Today*, 21 March 2012, https://www.indiatoday.in/india/north/story/when-a-kashmiri-teen-hijacked-plane-with-a-toy-pistol-96620-2012-03-21

Indian Defence News, 'The Ganga Hijack Drama: How RAW fooled Pakistan', https://defenceupdate.in/the-ganga-hijack-drama-how-raw-fooled-pakistan/

International Rescue Committee, *Escape from Terror, A Report of the International Rescue Committee Emergency Mission to India for Pakistan Refugees, submitted on 28 July 1971 by its Chairman Angier B. Duke to f.L Kellogg, Special Assistant to the Secretary of State for Refugee Affairs, Government of USA* (New York, NY: International Rescue Committee, 1971).

Isha Khan, 'India's RAW Operations in South Asian Countries', OpEd, *Eurasia Review*, 29 August 2012, https://www.eurasia review.com/29082012-indias-raw-operations-in-south-asian-countries-oped/

Ishfaq Ilahi Chowdhury, 'Indo-Pak War 1965: Looking Back 50 Years', *The Daily Star*, 22 September 2015, https://www.thedailystar.net/op-ed/politics/indo-pak-war-1965-146932; https://www.youtube.com/watch?v=hnL-jImAO28

Jairam Ramesh, *Intertwined Lives: P.N. Haksar and Indira Gandhi* (Simon & Schuster, New Delhi, 2018), pp. 204, 205, 209, 218, 230.

Jayshree Bajoria, 'RAW: India's External Intelligence Agency', 7 November 2008, https://www.cfr.org/backgrounder/raw-indias-external-intelligence-agency

K. Sankaran Nair, *Inside IB and RAW: The Rolling Stone that Gathered Moss* (Manas Publications, New Delhi, 2019).

Louis J. Smith, ed., *Foreign Relations of the United States, 1969–1976, South Asia Crisis, 1971*, United States Government Printing Office, 2005.

Lt. Gen. J.F.R Jacob, *An Odyssey in War and Peace* (Roli Books: 2011), p. 180.

Lt. Gen. J.F.R Jacob, *Surrender at Dhaka: Birth of a Nation* (The University Press Ltd, 1997), pp. 37, 41–3, 45, 53, 95, 101–30,134–46.

M. Waheeduzzaman Manik, The Historic Six-Point Movement and Its Impact on the Struggle for Independence, *The Daily Star*, 7 June 2008, https://www.thedailystar.net/news-detail-40021

M.N.R. Samant and Sandeep Unnithan, *Operation X: The Untold Story of India's Covert Naval War in East Pakistan* (HarperCollins Publishers India, 2019).

Maj Gen Sukhwant Singh, *India's Wars since Independence: The Liberation of Bangladesh* (Vikas Publishing House, New Delhi, 1991), pp. 49, 219.

Maj. Gen. P.K. Chakravorty (Retd), 'The Indo-Pak Bangladesh Liberation War, 1971' *India Strategic*, December 2011, https://www.indiastrategic.in/topstories1291_Indo-Pak_Bangladesh_liberation_war_1971.htm

Maj. Gen. Sukhwant Singh, 'East Pakistan: The Mukti Bahini Takes Shape', Book Excerpt: *India's War since Independence*, 3 March 2018, http://www.indiandefencereview.com/interviews/east-pakistan-the-mukti-bahini-takes-shape/

Maj. Gen. V.K. Singh, *India's External Intelligence: Secrets of Research and Analysis Wing* (Manas Publications, New Delhi, 2017).

Major Gazi Mohammed Tauhiduzzaman, 'Military Preparation for Operation Searchlight', *The Independent*, 26 March, 2016, http://www.theindependentbd.com/printversion/details/38507

Manu Pubby, 'India Loses 1971 War Hero; Declassified CIA Files Reveal Impact of His Operation Trident', *The Print*, 4 July 2017, https://theprint.in/report/india-loses-1971-war-hero-declassified-cia-files-reveal-impact-of-his-operation-trident/2024/

Mark Dummet, 'Bangladesh War: The Article That Made History', *BBC News*, 16 December 2011, https://www.bbc.com/news/world-asia-16207201

Md Nazrul Islam and Md Saidul Islam, *Islam and Democracy in South Asia: The Case of Bangladesh* (Palgrave Macmillan, USA, 2020).

Md Shahnawaz Khan Chandan, 'A History Written in Blood', *The Daily Star*, 16 December 2015, https://www.thedailystar.net/supplements/history-written-blood-187984

Md. Abdullah Al Zobair, 'Bangladesh Liberation War 1971', https://www.academia.edu/37201092/Liberation_War_of_Bangladesh

Moiz Abdul Majid, 'Ecologies of Emancipation: The Mukti Bahini, Rivers and the Unravelling of Pakistan', *Jamhoor*, 2 May 2020, https://www.jamhoor.org/read/2020/5/2/ecologies-of-emancipation-the-mukti-bahini-rivers-and-the-unravelling-of-pakistan

Namrata Goswami, 'Just War Theory and Humanitarian Intervention: A Comparative Study of East Pakistan and Kosovo', Jawaharlal Nehru University, Research Paper, Shodhganga, https://shodhganga.inflibnet.ac.in/handle/10603/18907

Naomi Hossain, 'The 1970 Bhola Cyclone, Nationalist Politics and the Subsistence Crisis Contract in Bangladesh', Institute of Development Studies, UK, 2017, https://www.ids.ac.uk/download.php?file=files/dmfile/Naomi_Hossain_Bhola_Cyclone_2017.pdf

Nuran Nabi, 'The Tangail Landings: A Signal for Victory', *The Daily Star*, 26 March 2015, https://www.thedailystar.net/supplements/independence-day-special-2015/the-tangail-landings-signal-victory-73754

Pakistan Defence, 'Indian R&AW's "Kao Plan" Unleashed in Balochistan', 13 May 2012, https://defence.pk/pdf/threads/indian-raws-kao-plan-unleashed-in-balochistan.179972/

Pankaj Mishra, 'Unholy Alliances: Nixon. Kissinger and the Bangladesh Genocide', *New Yorker*, 16 September 2013, https://www.newyorker.com/magazine/2013/09/23/unholy-alliances-3

Philip Hensher, 'The War Bangladesh Can Never Forget', *The Independent*, 19 February 2013, https://www.independent.co.uk/news/world/asia/the-war-bangladesh-can-never-forget-8501636.html

Praveen Swami, *India Pakistan and the Secret Jihad: The Covert War in Kashmir 1947–2004*, (Routledge, New York, 2006).

Praveen Swami, 'India's Secret War in Bangladesh', *The Hindu*, 26 December 2011, https://www.thehindu.com/opinion/lead/indias-secret-war-in-bangladesh/article2747538.ece

R.G. Kyle (Major, Royal Canadian Artillery), 'The India–Pakistan War of 1971: A Modern War', Marine Corps Command and Staff College—CSC 1984, https://www.globalsecurity.org/military/library/report/1984/KRG.htm

R.K. Yadav, *Mission R&AW* (Manas Publications, New Delhi, 2014), Chapters 8, 18.

Raghav Gakhar, 'How Two R&AW Agents Helped Indian Navy to Destroy Karachi Harbour in 1971 War', *Defencelover*, 28 November 2017, https://defencelover.in/two-raw-agents-helped-indian-navy-destroy-karachi-harbour-1971-war/

Rakesh Singh, 'China's PLA Learns Tamil, Malayalam to Intercept Indian Chatter', *The Sunday Standard*, 2 September 2017, https://www.newindianexpress.com/thesundaystandard/2017/sep/02/chinas-pla-learns-tamil-malayalam-to-intercept-indian-chatter-1651707.html

Ramamohan Rao, 'Role of Big Powers in Indo-Pak War of 1971' ANI, 15 December 2015, https://in.news.yahoo.com/role-big-powers-indo-pak-war-1971-032746121.html

Rasheed Kidwai, 'How the 1971 War was Fought and Won', 2 February 2019, https://www.orfonline.org/research/how-1971-war-fought-won

Ravi Shankar, 'The Secret Battlefield', *New Indian Express*, 10 June 2018, http://www.newindianexpress.com/magazine/2018/jun/10/the-secret-battlefield-1825074.html

Rinchen Norbu Wangchuk, 'How an Auschwitz Survivor Helped India Get Israel's Aid in the 1971 War', *The Better India*, 15 January 2018, https://www.thebetterindia.com/127816/auschwitz-survivor-india-israel-aid-1971-war/

Robert Jackson, *South Asian Crisis-India: Pakistan: Bangladesh* (Palgrave Macmillan, 1975), p. 171.

S.N. Prasad and U.P. Thapliyal, eds., *The India–Pakistan War of 1971: A History* (Natraj Publishers, Dehra Dun, 2014), pp. 45–58, 68, 72–73, 252–4, 341, 348, 364–5, 368–9, 375–7, 410

Saleem Samad, 'Remembering the "Phantoms of Chittagong"', *Dhaka Tribune*, 27 December 2019, https://www.dhakatribune.com/opinion/op-ed/2019/12/27/remembering-the-phantoms-of-chittagong

Salman Rushdie, *Shame* (Macmillan Education, UK, 1983).

Sanghamitra Mazumdar, 'International Mother Language Day, Ekushe February, Bangla and History of Bhasha Dibas', *The*

Statesman, 20 February 2019, https://www.thestatesman.com/
bengal/international-mother-language-day-ekushe-february-
bangla-history-bhasha-dibas-1502733796.html

Sanjay Mohanty, 'The United States Policy Towards India-
Pakistan Armed Conflicts', Jawaharlal Nehru University,
Research Paper, Shodhganga, https://shodhganga.inflibnet.ac.in/
handle/10603/19066

Sashanka S. Banerjee, 'The True Story of India's Decision to
Release 93,000 Pakistani POWs After 1971 War', *The Wire*, 26
March 2017, republished 2 March 2019, https://thewire.in/
history/the-untold-story-behind-indira-gandhis-decision-to-
release-93000-pakistani-pows-after-the-bangladesh-war

Shubhangi Pandey, US Sanctions on Pakistan and Their Failure
as Strategic Deterrent', Observer Research Foundation, 1 August
2018, https://www.orfonline.org/research/42912-u-s-sanctions-
on-pakistan-and-their-failure-as-strategic-deterrent/

Srinath Raghavan, *1971: A Global History of the Creation of
Bangladesh* (Harvard University Press, 2013).

Subir Bhaumik, 'The Ghosts of RAW', *The Opinion Pages*, 17
March 2017, https://opinion.bdnews24.com/2017/03/17/the-
ghosts-of-raw/

Sumit Walia, '1971 War: What Happened before Pakistan's Public
Surrender to India', *Sify*, –15 December 2017, https://www.sify.
com/news/1971-war-what-happened-before-pakistan-s-public-
surrender-to-india-news-columns-rmpqGydddeajd.html

Sydney H. Schanberg, 'He Tells Full Story of Arrest and
Detention', *The New York Times*, 18 January 1972, https://www.
nytimes.com/1972/01/18/archives/he-tells-full-story-of-arrest-
and-detention-sheik-mujib-describes.html

Syed Badrul Ahsan, 'Agartala Conspiracy Case Forty Years On',
The Daily Star, 18 June 2008, https://www.thedailystar.net/news-
detail-41580

The Daily Star, 'Righting the Grievous Wrong: His Life, Struggle',
The Daily Star, 19 November 2009, https://www.thedailystar.net/
august-15-special-coverage/his-life-struggle-1269613

The Daily Star, 'Tragic Events of 1971: Hamoodur Rahman Commission Report Excerpts', *The Daily Star*, https://www. thedailystar.net/sites/default/files/upload-2014/freedomintheair/ pdf/Hamoodur%20Rahman%20Commission%20Report_ Dawn%20(1).pdf

The Guardian, The Henderson Brooks–Bhagat Report, http:// www.indiandefencereview.com/wp-content/uploads/2014/03/ TopSecretdocuments2.pdf

The New York Times, *Mrs Gandhi Opens Talks with Mujib*, *The New York Times*, 7 February 1972, https://www.nytimes. com/1972/02/07/archives/mrs-gandhi-opens-talks-with-mujib-defense-and-economic-pact.html

The Times of India, 'Bhutan, Not India, Was First to Recognize Bangladesh', *The Times of India*, 9 December 2014, https:// timesofindia.indiatimes.com/world/south-asia/Bhutan-not-India-was-first-to-recognize-Bangladesh/articleshow/45434808. cms

The Week, 'Navy Day: How India Helped Change the Face of Naval Warfare', *The Week*, 4 December 2018, https://www. theweek.in/news/india/2018/12/04/navy-day-india-change-face-warfare.html

Vappala Balachandran, 'RN Kao, RAW's First Chief, Laid the Foundations of Indian Espionage', *Indian Express*, 20 August 2019, https://indianexpress.com/article/opinion/columns/rn-kao-raw-research-and-analysis-wing-5918230/

Vice Admiral (Retd) G. M. Hiranandani, *Transition to Triumph: Indian Navy 1956-1975* (Lancer Publishers, New Delhi: 2000), p. 142.

Vikas Vasudeva, 'Would Do it All Again', *The Hindu*, 20 January 2018, https://www.thehindu.com/news/national/will-do-it-all-again-says-punjab-spy-who-came-in-from-the-cold/article 22482714.ece

Acknowledgements

WRITING A BOOK IS HARD. WRITING A BOOK ABOUT THE SECRET services is harder. We embarked on this journey of our first book with a lot of trepidation. However, this odyssey was made a lot less challenging by Mr Hussain Zaidi's constant guidance and support. This book would not have been possible without his persistent nudging and encouragement. He followed up with us regularly even when we kept missing one deadline after another. He is the singular reason this book exists. Had he given up on us, this book would not have seen the light of day. In him, we have found a great friend, guide and mentor. We cannot thank you enough, Hussain sir.

Yogini Roygaga's dedication to her work is unwavering. She came on board as our researcher and assistant. She compiled copious amounts of research material, sorted it and worked on it tirelessly. She read and re-read every line of the book until she was satisfied with the material's authenticity. Without her, we would have been lost at sea. Her ever-smiling face made the work a lot less difficult.

A published fiction writer and journalist himself, Gautam S. Mengle eased us into the writing process. He drew from his writing experiences to give inputs on the shape and structure of chapters. He was a strong critic and a great sounding board.

We want to thank Mr Vappalla Balachandran for his time and insights into the world of espionage. He poured out his years of experience at the Indian secret services for us. Many of his anecdotes and experiences have made their way into the book.

We would especially like to thank Deepthi Talwar, our editor, who very patiently went through our drafts and helped make the book richer in every aspect.

We would also like to thank Golden Pen and Westland for showing trust in us.